Graphic Classics:
H.G. WELLS

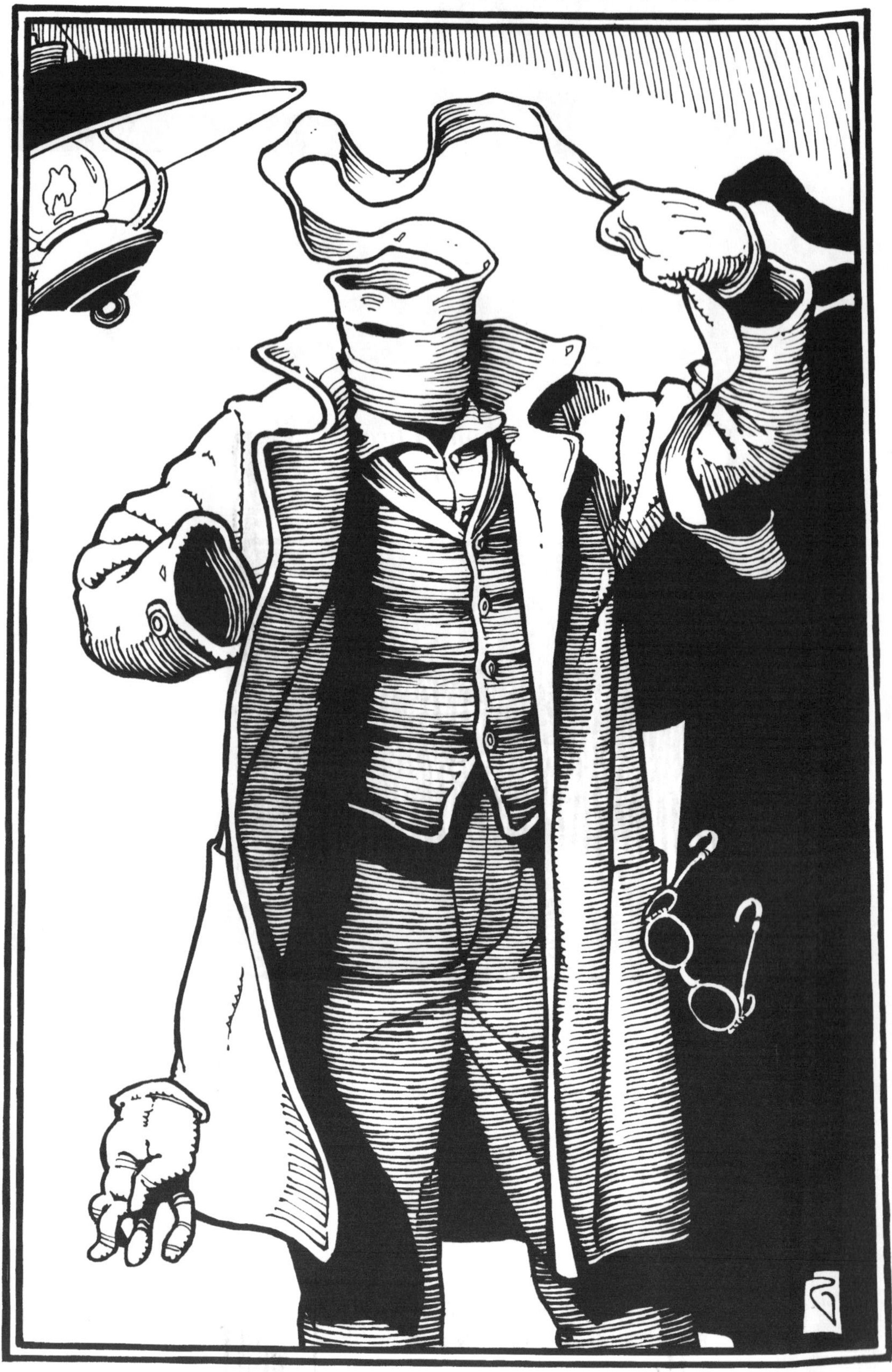

CONTENTS:

Graphic Classics: H.G. Wells is published by Eureka Productions. ISBN #0-9712464-3-2. Price US $9.95. Tom Pomplun, designer and publisher, tom@graphicclassics.com. Eileen Fitzgerald, editorial assistant. Available through The Rosebud Store, Eureka Productions, 8778 Oak Grove Road, Mount Horeb, WI 53572. The Graphic Classics website is at http://www.graphicclassics.com. Printed in USA. This compilation and all original works ©2002 Eureka Productions. All rights revert to creators after publication. Graphic Classics is a trademark of Eureka Productions.

Illustrations and comics: Cover ©1983 Vincent Di Fate / IFC ©1998 Spencer Walts / pages 1, 133-136 ©2002 Brad Teare / page 2 ©2002 Rick Geary / pages 7-39 ©1974 Educational Insights / pages 40-50, 139 ©2002 Dan O'Neill / pages 51-56 ©2002 Shary Flenniken / pages 58-61 ©2002 Skip Williamson / pages 62-76 ©1989 John Pierard / pages 77-85 ©2002 M.K. Brown / pages 86-96 ©2002 Nicola Cuti / pages 97-105 ©2002 Milton Knight / pages 106-124 ©2002 Sputnik Studios / pages 128-131 ©1997, 2000, 2001 Shag / pages 133-138 ©2002 Brad Teare / page 138 ©2002 Kent Steine / page 142 ©2002 Chris Moore / back cover ©2002 Jim Nelson.

Introduction ©2002 Ray Vukcevich. / Artwork for **The Invisible Man** by Alex Niño originally appeared in substantially different form in **The Invisible Man**, 1974, Pendulum Press. Reprinted by permission of Educational Insights, Rancho Dominguez, CA. Adaptation ©2002 Tom Pomplun. / **In the Abyss** originally appeared in **The Bank Street Book of Science Fiction** (Pocket Books, 1989). Reprinted by permission of the artist.

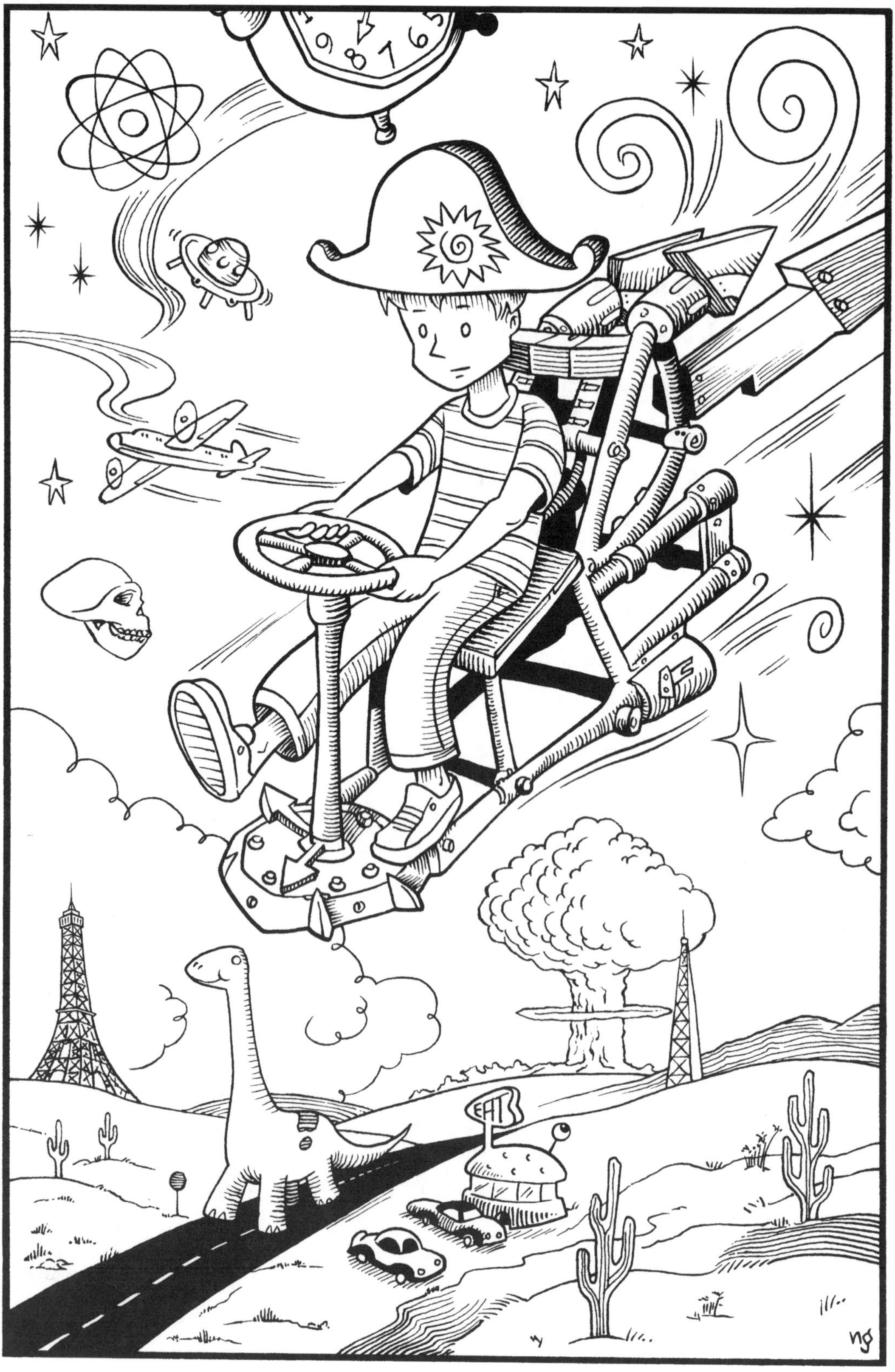

Build Your Own Time Machine!

by **Ray Vukcevich**

I think there were still canals on Mars when I was a kid. If there weren't, the news hadn't reached us yet in rural Arizona. We lived behind a mountain that mostly blocked the signal from Tucson, so we didn't have TV until around 1957 when my father got a huge set with a tiny round screen and ran a wire upstairs and hooked it to a clothes hanger which he then poked out a window. The picture was snowy but amazing. I remember what must have been drawings of Sputnik.

I didn't watch much TV on that little screen. Most of the images in my head from those days are from comic books. I remember seeing Martians with their long legs and one eye and the terrible beam they could shoot from the eye. And the guy riding the time machine.

I ordered the plans for an anti-gravity machine from an ad in the back of a comic book. It turned out you were supposed to construct a wheel with jars around the rim and fill some of the jars with water and spin the wheel and somehow the whole thing would lift off. You could strap it to your back and zoom around above the trees. The principle was probably related to the one people imagine using when in a falling elevator. You jump up and down because your odds of being up in the air when the elevator hits the ground are around 50/50, and if you're up in the air,

you only have a couple of feet to fall. Right?

Once built, the device lifted nothing no matter how fast you turned the crank and usually just slopped water all over the place, so I decided its true purpose must be to warp time.

We lived forty miles from the nearest real town in a place called Fort Grant. It was the state reform school for boys. The staff and their families lived on base. My father was the superintendent so we lived in the spooky old general's house. People said Geronimo had once been held captive there by the army. I don't know if that's true. The school was surrounded by a low rock wall that was always a work in progress. Outside of the wall and down a dirt road was a dump—not garbage, but great piles of junk—pipes and rolls of wire and glass insulators from the tops of telephone poles and boxes with switches and dials and old boards and broken bricks. I used to sneak out there and move the stuff I would need for my machines to a location further back in the wilderness, a secret meadow that I never showed anyone. This is where I built my time machine.

The time machine was made mainly from the same black metal pipes with flanges at one end that had been the propulsion system of an earlier spaceship. It just now hit me that a pipe like that might make interesting sounds if you blew into it like a didgeridoo; but I never did that. It's comforting to realize that I didn't use up all the possibilities of the situation the first time around.

The time machine was a folding metal chair with those black tubes arranged around it. I think there were five tubes sticking up out of the ground. There was a control panel made from a box with switches on the top and a dial at the side. The anti-gravity device (made from those little jars you used to get when you had a chemistry set)—now modified to warp time—was attached to the box like a steering wheel. Had I seen the movie, I might have put the wheel in the back, but the movie was still several years in the future. When you traveled in my machine you turned the wheel to the left to go into the past and to the right to go into the future. From the outside, it didn't look much like the machine in the classic comic book, but it was a different story from the inside.

A few years after I'd finished the machine, my father bought a dude ranch across the valley from the boys school. There were all these strange buildings made of adobe and in almost every building, dining room, bar, cabins, there were bookshelves and every shelf was filled to overflowing with books! I hadn't been in many libraries since we lived so far out in the sticks, so this was probably the biggest book collection I'd ever seen.

Here were Poe and Orwell and H. G. Wells. I first read *The Time Machine* and *The War of the Worlds* and *The Invisible Man* and *The Island of Dr. Moreau* at the ranch. I knew many of the stories from the comic books, but I was amazed at the books themselves. The images were already part of my makeup and now so were the words. In many ways, Wells is the first source of science fiction for me.

Another neat thing about the ranch was that Dick Calkins, the original artist for Buck Rogers, lived on ten acres just down the road. He had done many chalk sketches on the ranch walls. There were rocket ships and ray guns but also horses and six shooters. In one bathroom, for example, you'd see coming through a door drawn on the wall a grinning cowboy with a big brush saying something like, "Don't get up ma'am, I just come in to brush my tooth."

I would like to be able to report that I asked Dick Calkins for his take on the famous radio broadcast of the *War of the Worlds* by Orson Welles, but I only thought of that when it was much too late. At the time, I just didn't know to ask. Maybe I could go back to that secret meadow in the Graham Mountains and see if my time machine is still there and if it is, sit down and turn the wheel to the left.

In the meantime, though, I'll be reading Wells again and looking at all of these neat new pictures. I hope you'll join me for a good time. 🌹

The Invisible Man

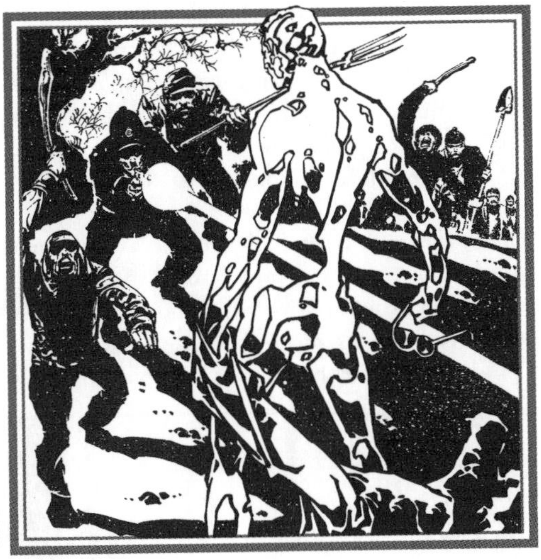

ILLUSTRATION ©1974 EDUCATIONAL INSIGHTS

illustrated by

ALEX NINO

Story by H.G. Wells

edited and abridged by Tom Pomplun

The stranger came early in February through a driving snow. He was wrapped from head to foot, and the brim of his hat hid every inch of his face but the shiny tip of his nose. He staggered into the Coach and Horses, more dead than alive as it seemed. "A fire," he cried, "in the name of human charity! A room and a fire!" And with that much introduction, and a couple of sovereigns flung upon the table, he took up his quarters in the inn.

Mrs. Hall lit the fire and went to prepare a meal. A guest to stop at Iping in the winter-time was an unheard-of piece of luck, and she was resolved to show herself worthy of her good fortune. Although the fire was burning up briskly, she was surprised to see that her visitor still wore his hat and coat, and was staring out of the window at the falling snow in the yard. "Can I take your hat and coat, sir," she said, "and give them a good dry in the kitchen?"

"I prefer to keep them on," he said, and she noticed that he wore big blue spectacles with side-lights and had a bushy side-whisker over his collar that hid his face.

"Very well, sir," she said. "In a bit the room will be warmer." He made no answer and Mrs. Hall laid the rest of the table things in a quick staccato and whisked out of the room.

When she returned with the breakfast, she noticed the overcoat and hat had been taken off and put over a chair in front of the fire. A pair of wet boots threatened rust to her steel fender.

"I suppose I may have them to dry now," she said in a voice that brooked no denial.

"Leave the hat," said her visitor in a muffled voice, and turning she saw he had raised his head and was looking at her. For a moment she stood gaping at him, too surprised to speak.

He held a cloth over the lower part of his face, so that his mouth was completely hidden. But it was not that which startled Mrs. Hall. It was the fact that all his forehead above his blue glasses was covered by a white bandage, leaving not a scrap of his face exposed except his pink, peaked nose. He wore a jacket with the collar turned up about his neck. Black hair, escaping below and between the cross bandages, projected in curious tails and horns, giving him the strangest appearance conceivable.

She placed the hat on the chair again by the fire. "I didn't know, sir," she began, "that—" and she stopped embarrassed.

"Thank you," he said drily.

She shivered as she closed the door. "The poor soul's had an accident or an op'ration or something," said Mrs. Hall. "What a turn them bandages did give me, to be sure!"

When Mrs. Hall later went to clear away the stranger's lunch, her idea that his mouth must also have been disfigured, was confirmed, for he was smoking a pipe, and all the time that she was in the room he never loosened the silk muffler he had wrapped round the lower part of his face to put the mouthpiece to his lips. He

sat in the corner and spoke with less aggressive brevity than before.

"I have some luggage," he said, "at Bramblehurst station," and he asked her how he could have it sent. "Tomorrow!" he said. "There is no speedier delivery?" and seemed quite disappointed when she answered "No."

"I should explain," he stated, "that I am an experimental investigator. My baggage contains apparatus and appliances, and I'm naturally anxious to get on with my inquiries."

"Of course, sir."

"My reason for coming to Iping," he proceeded, "was a desire for solitude. I do not wish to be disturbed. In addition to my work, an accident—necessitates a certain retirement. It is well these things should be understood."

"Certainly, sir," said Mrs. Hall. "And if I might make so bold as to ask—"

"That, I think, is all," said the stranger, with an air of finality. Mrs. Hall reserved her sympathy for a better occasion.

Mr. Hall on his return home was severely rated by his wife on the length of time he had spent in Sidderbridge, and his inquiries were answered snappishly. Hall resolved to ascertain more about the personality of his guest at the earliest possible opportunity. When retiring for the night he instructed Mrs. Hall to look very closely at the stranger's luggage when Fearenside delivered it next day.

"You mind your own business, Hall," said Mrs. Hall, "and I'll mind mine."

She was all the more inclined to snap because she was by no means assured about the stranger in her own mind. In the middle of the night she woke up dreaming of huge white heads with vast black eyes that came after her at the end of interminable necks.

Thus it was that this singular person fell out of infinity into Iping Village. Next day his luggage arrived. There were two trunks, a box of fat books, a dozen crates, and cases, containing objects packed in straw. The stranger came out impatiently to meet Fearenside's cart, not noticing the dog, who was sniffing at Hall's legs. "Come along with those boxes," he said. "I've been waiting long enough."

No sooner had Fearenside's dog caught sight of him, however, than it began to growl savagely, and it sprang straight at the stranger's leg. Then Fearenside's whip reached his property, and the dog yelped and retreated under

the wagon. Everyone shouted. The stranger glanced at his leg, then turned and rushed up the steps into the inn. They heard him go headlong across the passage and up the uncarpeted stairs to his bedroom.

Hall stood gaping. "He wuz bit, I'd better go and see," and he trotted after the stranger. He went straight upstairs, and the stranger's door being ajar, he pushed it open and entered. The blind was down and the room dim. He caught a glimpse of what seemed a handless arm waving towards him, and a face of three huge indeterminate spots on white. Then he was struck violently in the chest, hurled back, and the door slammed in his face and locked, all so rapidly that he had no time to observe. There he stood on the dark little landing, wondering what it might be that he had seen.

"He don't want no help, he says," Hall said in answer to his wife's enquiry. "We'd better be a-takin' of his luggage in."

Suddenly the dog growled again.

"Come along," cried an angry voice, and there stood the stranger. "The sooner you get those things in the better I'll be pleased."

"Was you hurt, sir?" said Fearenside. "I'm rare sorry the darg—"

"Not a bit," said the stranger. "Never broke the skin. Hurry with those things."

Directly the first crate was carried into the parlour, the stranger flung himself upon it and began to unpack. From it he began to produce bottles—little fat bottles containing powders, small and slender bottles containing coloured and white fluids, bottles with round bodies and slender necks, bottles with glass stoppers and frosted labels, bottles with fine corks, bottles with wooden caps—putting them in rows on the mantel, on the table under the window, round the floor — everywhere. Crate after crate yielded bottles, until all six were empty and the table high with straw; the only things that came out of these crates besides the bottles were a number of test-tubes and a carefully packed balance.

The stranger immediately set to work, not troubling in the least about the litter of straw, the books outside, nor for the trunks and other luggage that had gone upstairs.

When Mrs. Hall took his dinner to him, he was already so absorbed in his work, pouring little drops out of the bottles into test-tubes, that he did not hear her until she had swept away the bulk of the straw and put the tray on the table, with some little emphasis perhaps, seeing the state that the floor was in. Then he half turned his head and immediately turned it away again. But she saw he had removed his glasses, and it seemed to her that his eye sockets were extraordinarily hollow. He put on his spectacles again, and then turned and faced her.

"I wish you wouldn't come in without knocking," he said in his tone of abnormal exasperation.

10

"This stror, sir —"

"If the straw makes trouble put it down in the bill." And he mumbled at her—words suspiciously like curses.

All the afternoon he worked with the door locked and, as Mrs. Hall testifies, for the most part in silence. But once there was a concussion and a sound of bottles ringing together as though the table had been hit, and the smash of a bottle flung violently down. She went to the door and listened, not caring to knock.

"I can't go on," he was raving. "I can't go on. All my life it may take me! Patience indeed! Fool and liar!"

When she took in his tea she saw broken glass in the corner of the room, and a golden stain that had been carelessly wiped. She called attention to it.

"For God's sake don't worry me." snapped her visitor. "If there's damage done, put it down in the bill," and he went on ticking a list in the book before him.

Hall did not like the stranger, and he talked of getting rid of him; but he showed his dislike chiefly by concealing it ostentatiously, and avoiding his visitor as much as possible. There were a number of skirmishes with Mrs. Hall on matters of domestic discipline, but in every case until late in April, when the first signs of penury began, he overrode her by the easy expedient of an extra payment.

The stranger rarely went abroad by day, but at twilight he would go out muffled up, whether the weather were cold or not. He chose the loneliest paths and those most overshadowed by trees and banks. It was inevitable that a person of so remarkable an appearance and bearing should form a frequent topic in such a village as Iping. Opinion was greatly divided about his occupation. Mrs. Hall was sensitive on the point. Her visitor had had an accident, she said, which temporarily discoloured his face and hands; and being of a sensitive disposition, he was averse to any public notice of the fact.

Out of her hearing there was a view largely entertained that he was a criminal trying to escape from justice by wrapping himself up so as to conceal himself from the police. According to Mr. Gould, the stranger was an Anarchist in disguise, preparing explosives. Yet another view explained the entire matter by regarding the stranger as a harmless lunatic.

But whatever they thought of him, people in Iping on the whole agreed in disliking him. His irritability was an amazing thing to these quiet Sussex villagers. They drew aside as he passed down the village, and when he had gone by, young humorists would up with coat collars and down with hat brims, and go pacing nervously after him in imitation of his occult bearing calling "Bogey Man!"

Cuss, the general practitioner, was devoured by curiosity. The bandages excited his professional interest, and the report of the thousand and one bottles aroused his jealous regard. All through April and May he coveted an opportunity of talking to the stranger; and at last he could stand it no longer. He was surprised to find that Mr. Hall did not know his guest's name. "He give a name," said Mrs. Hall—an assertion which was quite unfounded—"but I didn't rightly hear it."

Cuss rapped at the parlour door and entered. "Pardon my intrusion," he said, and then the door closed and cut Mrs. Hall off from the rest of the conversation. She could hear the murmur of voices for the next ten minutes, then a cry of surprise, quick steps to the door, and Cuss appeared, his face white, his eyes staring over his shoulder. He strode across the hall and down the steps, and she heard his feet hurrying along the road. Then she heard the stranger laughing quietly. The parlour door slammed, and the place was silent again.

Cuss went straight to Bunting the vicar. "Am I mad?" Cuss began abruptly. "Do I look like an insane person?"

When his nerves had been steadied by a glass of sherry he told him of the interview he had just had. "Went in," he gasped, "and asked him, was he researching. Said he was. A long research? Got quite cross. 'A damnable long research,' said he. The man was just on the boil, and my question boiled him over. 'Damn you! What are you fishing after?' I apologised. Just at that point, out came his arm."

"Well?"

"No hand—just an empty sleeve. Lord! There was nothing in it, I tell you. Nothing down it, right down to the joint. 'Good God!' I said. Then he stared at me with those black goggles of his."

"Well?"

"That's all. He never said a word; just glared, and put his sleeve back in his pocket quickly. 'How the devil,' said I, 'can you move an empty sleeve like that?'

"'It's an empty sleeve, is it?' He came towards me slowly. Then very quietly he pulled his sleeve out of his pocket and raised his arm towards me. I was beginning to feel frightened. I could see right down it. He extended it straight towards me, until the cuff was six

inches from my face. And then—"

"Well?"

"Something—exactly like a finger and thumb it felt—nipped my nose."

Bunting began to laugh.

"There wasn't anything there!" shrieked Cuss. "It's all very well for you to laugh, but I tell you I was so startled, I hit his cuff hard and cut out of the room—" Cuss stopped. There was no mistaking the sincerity of his panic. "When I hit his cuff, it felt exactly like hitting an arm. And there wasn't an arm!"

Mr. Bunting looked suspiciously at Cuss. "It's really," said Bunting with judicial emphasis, "a most remarkable story."

The facts of the burglary at the vicarage came to us chiefly through the medium of the vicar and his wife. Mrs. Bunting, it seems, woke up before the dawn, with the strong impression that the door of their bedroom had opened and closed. She then heard the pad of bare feet walking along the passage towards the staircase. She aroused the Rev. Mr. Bunting as quietly as possible. He did not strike a light, but went out on the landing to listen. He heard a fumbling going on at his study desk downstairs. At that he returned to his bedroom, armed himself with the poker, and descended the staircase as noiselessly as possible.

Everything was still except the creaking of the stairs under Mr. Bunting's tread, and the slight movements in the study. Through the crack of the door he could see a candle burning on the desk, but the robber he could not see. He heard the chink of money, and realised that the robber had found the housekeeping reserve. At that sound Mr. Bunting was nerved to action. Gripping the poker, he rushed into the room, followed by Mrs. Bunting. "Surrender!" cried Mr. Bunting, and then stopped amazed. The room was perfectly empty.

Yet their conviction that they had heard somebody moving in the room had amounted to a certainty. Mrs. Bunting went across the room and looked behind the screen, while Mr. Bunting peered under the desk. Then Mrs. Bunting turned back the curtains, and Mr. Bunting looked up the chimney and probed it with the poker. Then Mrs. Bunting scrutinised the wastepaper basket and Mr. Bunting opened the lid of the coal scuttle.

"I could have sworn—" said Mr. Bunting.

"The candle!" said Mrs. Bunting. "Who lit the candle? And the money's gone!"

There was a sneeze in the passage. They rushed out, and as they did so the kitchen door slammed. The place was empty. There was not a soul to be found in the house, search as they would. Daylight found the vicar and his wife still marvelling about by the unnecessary light of a guttering candle.

Now it happened that in the early hours of that day, Mr. and Mrs. Hall were in the cellar. Their business there was of a private nature, and had something to do with the specific gravity of their beer. Mrs. Hall found she had forgotten to bring down a bottle of sarsaparilla and sent Hall upstairs for it.

On the landing he was surprised to see that the stranger's door was ajar. Returning with

the bottle, he noticed that the bolts of the front door had been shot back. He rapped at the stranger's door. There was no answer. He rapped again; then entered. On the bedroom chair and along the rail of the bed were the garments and the bandages of their guest.

As Hall stood there he heard his wife's voice coming out of the cellar and he hurried down to her. "Janny," he said, over the rail of the cellar steps, "'E's not in uz room, 'e ent. And the front door's unbolted."

Mrs. Hall resolved to see the room for herself. "If 'e ent there," Hall said, "his close are. And what's 'e doin' without his close, then?"

Mrs. Hall ran upstairs. She flung open the door and stood regarding the room. She bent forward and put her hand on the pillow and then under the clothes. "Cold," she said. "He's been up this hour or more."

As she did so, the bedclothes gathered themselves, leapt up suddenly, and then jumped headlong over the bottom rail. The stranger's hat hopped off the bedpost and dashed straight at Mrs. Hall's face. Then as swiftly came the sponge from the washstand. Then the chair turned itself up with its legs at Mrs. Hall, seemed to take aim at her for a moment, then charged. She screamed and turned, as the chair legs came gently but firmly against her back and impelled her and Hall out of the room. The door slammed violently and was locked.

Mrs. Hall was left almost in a fainting condition in Mr. Hall's arms on the landing. "Lock him out," she said. "Don't let him come in again. I might ha' known. With them goggling eyes and bandaged head, and never going to church of a Sunday. And all they bottles, he's put the sperrits into the furniture. My good old furniture! 'Twas in that very chair my dear mother used to sit when I was a girl. To think it should rise up against me now!"

It took some time for the landlady's husband to work up his nerve. At last he opened the door, and got as far as, "Excuse me—"

"Go to the devil!" said the stranger in a tremendous voice, and "Shut that door after you." So that brief interview terminated.

The stranger remained in the parlour until near midday, the blinds down, the door shut, and none, after Hall's repulse, venturing near him.

Thrice he rang his bell, but no one answered him. "Him and his 'go to the devil' indeed!" said Mrs. Hall. Presently came rumour of the burglary at the vicarage, and two and two were put together. Hall went off to find the magistrate. No one ventured upstairs.

A group of scared but curious people increased. And in the darkness of the parlour, the stranger, hungry we must suppose, hidden in his wrappings, pored through his dark glasses upon his paper or chinked his dirty little bottles, and occasionally swore savagely. About noon he suddenly opened the parlour door and stood glaring fixedly at the people in the bar. "Mrs. Hall," he said. Somebody went sheepishly and called for Mrs. Hall.

Mrs. Hall appeared after an interval, holding a little tray with an unsettled bill upon it. "Is it your bill you're wanting, sir?" she said.

"Why wasn't my breakfast laid? Why haven't you prepared my meals and answered my bell?

"Why isn't my bill paid?" said Mrs. Hall. "That's what I want to know."

"I told you I was awaiting a remittance—"

"You can't grumble if your breakfast waits a bit, if my bill's been waiting these five days, can you?"

"I daresay in my pocket—"

"You told me two days ago that you hadn't anything—"

"Well, I've found some more—"

"I wonder where you found it!" said Mrs. Hall. "And before I take any bills or get any breakfasts, or do any such things whatsoever, you got to tell me one or two things I don't understand, and what nobody don't understand, and what everybody is very anxious to understand. I want know what you been doing t' my chair upstairs, and I want know how 'tis your room was empty, and how you got in again. And I want know—"

Suddenly the stranger raised his hands and said, "Stop!" with such violence that he silenced her instantly.

"You don't understand," he said, "who I am or what I am. I'll show you!" Then he put his hand over his face and withdrew it. "Here," he said. He stepped forward and handed Mrs. Hall something which she, staring, accepted automatically. Then, when she saw what it was, she screamed loudly, dropped it, and staggered back. The nose—it was the stranger's nose!—rolled on the floor.

Then he removed his spectacles, and everyone in the bar gasped. He took off his hat, and with a violent gesture tore at his whiskers and bandages. "Oh, my Gard!" said someone.

It was worse than anything. Mrs. Hall, standing open-mouthed and horror-struck, shrieked at what she saw, and made for the door of the house. They were prepared for scars, disfigurements, but nothing! Everyone tumbled on everyone else down the steps. For the man who stood there was a solid

gesticulating figure up to the collar of him, and then—nothingness, no visible thing at all!

People down the village heard shouts, and saw the Coach and Horses violently firing out its humanity. Then they heard the frightful screams of Millie, who, emerging from the kitchen at the noise, had come upon the headless stranger from behind.

In its struggles to see in through the open door, a crowd formed. There was a disturbance behind, and a little procession marched resolutely towards the house—first Mr. Hall, then Mr. Bobby Jaffers, the village constable, and then the wary Mr. Wadgers. They had come armed with a warrant.

Mr. Hall marched up the steps, straight to the door of the parlour and flung it open. "Constable," he said, "do your duty."

Jaffers marched in, He saw in the dim light the headless figure facing them, with a crust of bread in one gloved hand and a chunk of cheese in the other.

"What the devil's this?" came a tone of angry expostulation from above the collar of the figure.

"You're a damned rum customer, mister," said Mr. Jaffers. "But 'ed or no 'ed, duty's duty—"

"Keep off!" said the figure, starting back. Abruptly he whipped down the bread and cheese. Off came the stranger's glove and was slapped in Jaffers' face. In another moment Jaffers had gripped him by the handless wrist and caught his invisible throat. "I'll surrender," cried the stranger, and in another moment he stood up panting, a strange figure, headless and handless—for he had pulled off his other glove. The stranger ran his arm down his waistcoat, and as if by a miracle the buttons to which his empty sleeve pointed became undone. The suit of clothes stood, arms akimbo. Several other of the men folks had now entered the room, so that it was closely crowded. "Why am I assaulted by a policeman in this fashion?"

"No doubt you are a bit difficult to see in this light," said Jaffers, "but I got a warrant. What I'm after ain't no invisibility—it's burglary. There's a house been broken into and money took."

"Stuff and nonsense!" said the Invisible Man.

"I hope so, sir; but I've got my instructions."

Before anyone could realise what was being done, the stranger's slippers, socks, and trousers had been kicked off. Then he flung off his coat.

"Here, stop that," said Jaffers, suddenly realising what was happening. He gripped the waist-coat; it struggled, and the shirt slipped out of it and left it limp and empty in his hand. "Hold him!" said Jaffers loudly. "Once he gets they things off—!"

"Hold him!" cried everyone, and there was a rush at the fluttering white shirt which was now all that was visible of the stranger. "Look out! Hold him! Don't let him loose!" said everybody, fencing at random and hitting nothing.

"I got him!" shouted Jaffers, wrestling with purple face against his unseen enemy.

Men staggered right and left as the extraordinary conflict swayed swiftly towards the house door, and went spinning down the steps of the inn. Jaffers, holding tight, spun round, and fell heavily with his head on the gravel. Only then did his fingers relax.

Across the road, a woman screamed as something pushed by her; a dog, kicked apparently, yelped and ran into Huxter's yard, and with that the transit of the Invisible Man was accomplished. For a space people stood amazed, and then came panic, which scattered them abroad as a gust scatters dead leaves.

Mr. Thomas Marvel was sitting with his bare feet in a ditch, about a mile and a half out of Iping. In a leisurely manner—he did everything in a leisurely manner—he was contemplating trying on a pair of boots. They were the soundest boots he had come across for a long time, but too large for him; whereas the ones he had were a very comfortable fit, but too thin-soled for damp. Mr. Marvel hated roomy boots, but then he hated damp. He had never properly thought out which he hated most, so he put the four boots in a graceful group on the turf and looked at them. He was not at all startled by a voice behind him.

"They're boots, anyhow," said the voice.

"They are—charity boots," said Mr. Thomas Marvel, regarding them distastefully. "I've got my boots in this county ten years or more. And then they treat you like this."

"It's a beast of a county," said the voice. "And pigs for people."

Mr. Marvel turned to look at the boots of his interlocutor and lo! where boots should have been were neither legs nor boots. "Am I drunk?" he asked. "Have I had visions?"

"You think I'm just imagination?"

"What else can you be?" said Mr. Marvel, rubbing the back of his neck.

"It's very simple," said the voice. "I'm an invisible man. What I want to say at present is this: I need help. I have come to that. I was wandering, mad with rage, naked, impotent. Then I saw you and stopped. 'Here,' I said, 'is an outcast like myself. This is the man for me.'"

"Lord!" said Mr. Marvel. "And what may you be requiring in the way of help?"

"I want you to help me get clothes—and shelter—and then, other things. If you won't—well! But you will—must."

"Look here," said Mr. Marvel. "Don't knock me about anymore. It's all so unreasonable. Nothing visible for miles except the bosom of Nature. And then comes a voice out of heaven! And a fist—"

"Pull yourself together," said the voice, "for you have to do the job I've chosen for you. You are the only man, except some of those fools down there, who knows there is such a thing as an invisible man. Help me, and I will do great things for you. An invisible man is a man of power," he said, "But if you betray me—"

Mr. Marvel gave a yelp of terror at his touch. "I don't want to betray you—just tell me what I got to do. Whatever you want done, that I'm most willing to do."

After the first gusty panic had spent itself Iping became argumentative. It is so much easier not to believe in an invisible man; and those who had actually seen him dissolve into air, or felt the strength of his arm, could be counted on the fingers of two hands. By the afternoon even those who believed in the unseen were beginning to resume their amusements in a tentative fashion, on the supposition that he had quite gone away, and with the skeptics he was already a jest. About four o'clock a stranger in a shabby top hat entered the village. He turned the corner by the church, and directed his way to the Coach and Horses.

This stranger appeared to be talking to himself. He stopped at the foot of the steps, and appeared to undergo a severe internal struggle before he could induce himself to enter. Finally he marched up the steps, and was seen to turn to the left and open the door of the parlour. "That room's private!" said Hall, and the stranger shut the door clumsily and went into the bar. In the course of a few minutes he reappeared, wiping his lips with the back of his hand with an air of quiet satisfaction. He stood looking about him for some moments, and then Mr. Huxter, the tobacconist, saw him walk in an oddly furtive manner towards the gates of the yard. The stranger leaned against one of the gateposts, and produced a short clay pipe. Folding his arms, he began to smoke in a languid attitude, an attitude which his occasional quick glances up the yard altogether belied.

All this Mr. Huxter saw over the canisters of the tobacco window, and the singularity of the man's behaviour prompted him to maintain his observation.

At that same time Mr. Cuss and Mr. Bunting were in the parlour of the inn, making an examination of the Invisible Man's belongings. The stranger's garments had been removed by Mrs. Hall and the room tidied up. And on the table under the window Cuss had hit almost at once on three books in manuscript labeled DIARY.

"Diary!" said Cuss, putting the books on the table. "Now, at any rate, we shall learn something." He turned the pages with a face suddenly disappointed. "It's all cypher, Bunting."

The door opened suddenly.

Both gentlemen started, then were relieved to see a rosy face beneath a silk hat. "Tap?" asked the face, and stood staring.

"Over the other side," said Mr. Bunting.

"Please shut that door," said Cuss irritably.

"One thing is indisputable," said Bunting, drawing up a chair next to that of Cuss. "There certainly have been strange things happening in Iping during the last few days. I cannot of course believe this absurd invisibility story—"

Suddenly he became aware of a strange feeling at the nape of his neck, the grip of a heavy, firm hand, which bore his chin irresistibly to the table. "Don't move, little men," whispered a voice, "or I'll brain you both! Since when did you learn to pry into an investigator's private memoranda?" and two chins struck the table simultaneously. "Since when did you learn to invade the private rooms of a man in misfortune?" and the concussion was repeated.

"Where have they put my clothes?" said the voice. "I am a strong man—besides being invisible. There's not the slightest doubt that I could kill you both and get away—do you understand? Very well. If I let you go will you promise to do what I tell you?"

"Yes," said Mr. Bunting, and the Doctor repeated it. Then the pressure on the necks relaxed, and the Doctor and the Vicar sat up, both very red in the face.

"Please keep sitting where you are. When I came into this room," said the Invisible Man, "I expected to find, in addition to my books of memoranda, an outfit of clothing. Now, just at present, though the days are quite warm enough for an invisible man to run about stark, the evenings are chilly. I want clothing—and I must also have those three books."

While these things were going on in the parlour, and while Mr. Huxter was watching Mr. Marvel smoking his pipe against the gate, not a dozen yards away were Mr. Hall

and Teddy Henfrey discussing in a state of cloudy puzzlement the one Iping topic. Suddenly there came a thud against the door of the parlour, a sharp cry, and then—silence.

"Hsh!" said Henfrey. "Didn't I hear the window?"

Everyone stood listening. Mrs. Hall saw the oblong of the inn door, the road white and vivid, and Huxter's shop-front blistering in the June sun. Abruptly the door opened and Huxter appeared, arms gesticulating. "Stop thief!" he cried, and ran towards the gates.

As he did so, Mr. Marvel reappeared, his hat askew, a big bundle in one hand, and three books tied together in the other. Directly he saw Huxter he gave a gasp, and began to run. "Stop!" cried Huxter, and set off after him. He had hardly gone ten strides before his shin was caught in some mysterious fashion, and he was no longer running, but flying through the air.

Hall, Henfrey, and the human contents of the tap rushed out into the street. They saw someone whisk round the corner towards the down road, and Mr. Huxter executing a complicated leap in the air that ended on his face and shoulder.

Hall and two labourers from the tap rushed to the corner and saw Mr. Marvel running by the church wall. They jumped to the conclusion that this was the Invisible Man suddenly become visible, and set off in pursuit. But Hall had hardly run a dozen yards before he gave a shout and went flying headlong, clutching one of the labourers and bringing him to the ground. The second labourer came round, only

to be tripped just as Huxter had been.

When Hall and the others ran out of the house, Mrs. Hall, disciplined by years of experience, remained in the bar next to the till. Suddenly the parlour door was opened, and Mr. Cuss appeared. He rushed down the steps. "Hold him!" he bawled. "He's got my trousers! And every stitch of the Vicar's clothes!"

Cuss was promptly knocked off his feet into an indecorous sprawl. He yelled, struggled to regain his feet, was knocked on all fours again, and became aware that he was involved not in a capture, but a rout.

The Invisible Man's original intention was simply to cover Marvel's retreat with the clothes and books. But his temper, at no time very good, seems to have gone completely, and he set to smiting for the mere satisfaction of hurting.

The street was full of running figures, of doors slamming and fights for hiding-places. And then the whole tumultuous rush had passed and the Iping street was deserted save for the still raging unseen.

The Invisible Man amused himself for a little while by breaking all the windows in the Coach and Horses, and then he thrust a street lamp through the parlour window of Mrs. Gribble. He cut the telegraph wire to Adderdean, and after that he was neither heard, seen, nor felt in Iping. He vanished absolutely.

But it was the best part of two hours before any human being ventured out again into the desolation of Iping Street.

Ten o'clock the next morning found Mr. Marvel sitting with the books beside him, looking very weary and uncomfortable, on the bench outside a little inn on the outskirts of Port Stowe. His hands would go ever and again to his various pockets with a curious fumbling.

When he had been sitting for an hour, however, an elderly mariner, carrying a newspaper, came and sat down beside him. "Pleasant day," said the mariner.

Mr. Marvel glanced about him with something very like terror. "Very," he said.

As the mariner had approached Mr. Marvel he had heard a sound like the dropping of coins into a pocket. He was struck by the contrast of Mr. Marvel's appearance with this suggestion of opulence. Thence his mind wandered back again to a topic that had taken a curiously firm hold of his imagination.

"There's a story in this newspaper," said the mariner, "about an Invisible Man."

"An Invisible Man!" said Mr. Marvel. "And what's he been up to?"

"Iping's the place he started at," said the mariner. "And where he came from, nobody don't seem to know. Here it is: *Pe Culiar Story from Iping.* And it says in this paper there is a clergyman and a medical gent witnesses—saw 'im all right and proper'—or leastways, didn't see 'im. *In an alteration in the inn, his bandages was torn off. It was then ob-served that his head was invisible.*"

"He didn't have any pals—it don't say he had any pals, does it?" asked Mr. Marvel.

"Ain't one enough for you?" asked the mariner. "No, thank Heaven, he didn't. *He is at present at large, and it is supposed that he took the road to Port Stowe. You see we're right in it!*"

All this time Mr. Marvel had been glancing about, listening for faint footfalls, trying to detect imperceptible movements. He looked about him again, listened, bent towards to the mariner, and lowered his voice: "The fact of it is—I happen—to know just a thing or two about this Invisible Man." Suddenly his expression changed marvelously. "Ow!" he said. He rose stiffly in his seat.

"What's up?" said the mariner.

"Toothache," said Mr. Marvel, and put his hand to his ear. He caught hold of his books. "I must be getting on, I think," he said. He edged in a curious way along the seat.

"But you was just agoing to tell me about this Invisible Man!" protested the mariner.

"Hoax," said a voice.

"It's a hoax," said Mr. Marvel.

"But it's in the paper," said the mariner.

"Hoax all the same," said Marvel. "There ain't no Invisible Man whatsoever—blimey."

"Then why did you let me go on and tell you all this blarsted stuff, then? What d'yer mean by letting a man make a fool of himself like that for?"

Mr. Marvel suddenly whirled about and marched off in a curious spasmodic manner, with occasional violent jerks forward.

"Silly devil!" said the mariner, watching the receding figure. "I'll show you, you silly ass— hoaxing me! It's here—on the paper!"

And there was another extraordinary thing the mariner was presently to hear, and that was a vision of a "fist full of money" travelling without visible agency, along the wall at the corner of St. Michael's Lane. A brother mariner had seen this wonderful sight that very morning. He had snatched at the money and had been

knocked headlong, and when he had got to his
feet the butterfly money had vanished.

The story of the flying money was true. All
about that neighbourhood, from the tills of
shops and inns money had been making off that
day in handfuls, floating quietly along by walls
and shady places, dodging quickly from the approaching eyes of men. And it had, though no
man had traced it, invariably ended its flight in
the pocket of that agitated gentleman in the
obsolete hat, sitting outside the inn on the outskirts of Port Stowe.

In the early evening Doctor Kemp was
sitting in his study overlooking Burdock.
His eye presently wandering from his work
caught the sunset blazing at the back of the hill
that is over against his own. And then his attention was attracted by the figure of a man
running over the hill towards him. "Another
of those fools," said Doctor Kemp. "Like that
ass who ran into me this morning round a corner, with his "Visible Man a-coming, sir!' I
can't imagine what possesses people. One
might think we were in the thirteenth century."

But those who saw the fugitive nearer, and
perceived the abject terror on his face, did not
share in the doctor's contempt. All he passed
began staring up the road and down, and inter-
rogating one another for the reason of his haste.

The Jolly Cricketers is at the bottom of the
hill, where the tram-lines begin. Footsteps approached, running heavily, the door
was opened violently, and Marvel, weeping and
dishevelled, rushed in, made a convulsive turn,
and attempted to shut the door. It was held
half-open by a strap. "He's coming!" he bawled,
his voice shrieking with terror. "The 'Visible
Man! After me! For Gawd's sake! Elp!"

"Who's coming? What's the row?" said a
policeman. He went to the door, released the
strap, and it slammed.

"Lemme go inside," said Marvel, staggering and weeping, but still clutching the books.
"Lock me in somewhere. He's after me. I give
him the slip. He said he'd kill me and he will."

"You're safe," said a man with a black beard.
"What's it all about?"

Marvel shrieked as a blow suddenly made
the fastened door shiver. "Hullo," cried the
policeman, "who's there?"

Mr. Marvel rushed behind the bar. "Don't open the door," he cried.

The window of the inn was suddenly smashed in, and there was a screaming and running in the street. "I wish I had my truncheon," said the policeman, going irresolutely to the door.

"Draw the bolts," said the man with the black beard, "and if he comes —" He showed a revolver in his hands.

"Not with that thing going off behind me," said the barman.

"Very well," said the man with the black beard, and gun ready, drew them himself. Barman, cabman, and policeman faced about.

"Come in," said the bearded man in an undertone, standing back and facing the unbolted doors. "He's going round," cried Marvel. "He's as artful as the devil." Suddenly the bar-parlour door burst open. They heard Marvel squeal like a caught leveret. The bearded man's gun cracked and the looking-glass at the back of the parlour came smashing down.

Marvel struggled against the door that led to the yard and kitchen. The door flew open, and he was dragged through. Then the policeman rushed in, followed by one of the cabmen, and gripped the wrist of the invisible hand that collared Marvel. He was hit in the face and went reeling back. "I got him," said the cabman. The barman's red hands came clawing at the unseen. "Here he is!" said the barman.

Marvel, released, suddenly dropped to the ground and made an attempt to crawl behind the legs of the fighting men. The Invisible Man yelled out sharply, as the policeman trod on his foot. Then his fists flew round like flails. The cabman suddenly doubled up, kicked under the diaphragm. The door into the bar-parlour slammed and covered Mr. Marvel's retreat. The men in the kitchen found themselves clutching at and struggling with empty air.

"Where's he gone?" cried the bearded man.

"This way," said the policeman, stepping into the yard and stopping.

A piece of tile whizzed by his head and smashed among the crockery on the table.

"I'll show him," shouted the man with the black beard, and suddenly five bullets had followed one another into the twilight whence the missile had come. As he fired, the man moved his hand in a horizontal curve, so that his shots radiated out into the narrow yard like spokes from a wheel. A silence followed. "Five cartridges," said the bearded man. "Get a lantern, someone, and feel about for his body."

Doctor Kemp had continued writing in his study until the shots aroused him. It must have been about an hour after this that the doorbell rang. He heard the servant answer the door, and waited for her feet on the staircase, but she did not come. He went to the landing and called to the maid below. "Was that a letter?" he asked.

"A runaway ring, sir," she answered.

He went back to his study, and attacked his work resolutely. It was two o'clock before Doctor Kemp had finished for the night. He rose, yawned, and went downstairs to bed.

As he crossed the hall, he noticed a dark spot on the linoleum near the mat at the foot of the stairs, and bending down, found it had the stickiness and colour of drying blood.

He returned upstairs, looking about him and trying to account for the spot. On the

landing he stopped, astonished. The door handle of his own room was blood-stained.

He remembered that the door had been
open when he came down from his study. He
went straight into his room —perhaps a trifle
more resolute than usual. On the counterpane
was a mess of blood, and the bedsheet had been
torn. The bedclothes were depressed as if
someone had been recently sitting there.

Then he had an odd impression that he had
heard a voice say, "Good Heavens!—Kemp!"
But Doctor Kemp was no believer in voices.

He closed the door of the room and put
down his burdens. Suddenly, with a start, he
perceived a blood-stained bandage hanging in
mid-air between him and the washstand.

"Kemp!" said a voice.

"Eigh?" said Kemp, his mouth open.

"Keep your nerve," said the voice. "I'm an
Invisible Man."

The story he had ridiculed only that morning rushed through Kemp's brain. "I thought
it was all a lie," he said. "But this is some trick."
He stepped forward and his hand, extended
towards the bandage, met invisible fingers. He
recoiled at the touch.

"Keep steady, Kemp, for God's sake! I want
help badly. Stop!"

A hand gripped his arm. He was suddenly
tripped and flung backwards upon the bed. He
opened his mouth to shout, and the corner of
the sheet was thrust between his teeth.

"Listen to reason, will you?" bawled the
Invisible Man in Kemp's ear. "I'm an Invisible
Man. It's no foolishness, and no magic. I don't
want to hurt you, but if you behave like a fran-
tic rustic, I must. Don't you remember me,
Kemp?—Griffin, of University College?"

"Griffin?" said Kemp.

"I am Griffin. I am a man you have
known—made invisible. I'm wounded and in
pain, and tired. Give me some food and drink,
and let me sit down here."

Kemp stared at the bandage as it crossed
the room, then saw a chair dragged across the
floor and come to rest near the bed. It creaked,
and the seat was depressed the quarter of an
inch or so. He rubbed his eyes and felt his
neck. "This beats ghosts," he said, and laughed
stupidly.

"That's better. You're getting sensible! Give
me some whisky. I'm near dead."

"It didn't feel so. Whisky? Here."

The chair creaked and Kemp felt the glass drawn away from him. It came to rest poised above the chair.

I'm starving," said the voice, "and the night is chilly to a man without clothes. Have you got a dressing gown?"

Kemp walked to a wardrobe and produced a dingy robe. It hung limp for a moment in mid-air, fluttered weirdly, buttoned itself, and sat down in his chair. "Drawers, socks, slippers would be a comfort," said the unseen, curtly. "And food."

Kemp turned out his drawers for the articles, and then went downstairs to ransack his larder. He came back with some cold cutlets and bread, pulled up a light table, and placed them before his guest.

"I always like to get something about me before I eat," said the Invisible Man, with a full mouth, eating greedily. "It's odd I should blunder into your house to get my bandaging. My first stroke of luck. It's a filthy nuisance, my blood showing, isn't it? Gets visible as it coagulates, I see."

"But how's it done?" began Kemp, in exasperation. "The whole business—it's unreasonable from beginning to end."

"Quite reasonable," said the Invisible Man. "Perfectly reasonable."

Kemp stared at the devouring dressing gown. "What were the shots?" he asked.

"There was a man—a sort of confederate—who tried to steal my money."

"You didn't do any shooting?"

"Not me," said the visitor. "Some fool I'd never seen fired at random. They all got scared at me. Curse them!"

After he had done eating the Invisible Man demanded a cigar. It was strange to see him smoking; his mouth and throat became visible as a whirling smoke cast. "I'm lucky to have fallen upon you, Kemp. I'm in a devilish scrape. But we will do things yet. Let me tell you—"

"But how was it all done?" said Kemp, "and how did you get like this?"

"For God's sake, let me smoke in peace for a while! And then I will tell you."

But the story was not told that night. The Invisible Man's wrist was growing painful. He groaned suddenly and leaned forward, supporting his invisible head on invisible hands.

"Kemp," he said, "I've had no sleep for three days. Oh, God! How I want sleep!"

"Why not?"

The Invisible Man appeared to be regarding Kemp. "Because, I've a particular objection to being caught by my fellow-men," he said slowly.

Exhausted as the Invisible Man was, he refused to accept Kemp's word that his freedom should be respected. He examined the windows, drew the blinds, and opened the sashes to confirm Kemp's statement that a retreat would be possible. Finally he expressed himself satisfied.

"I'm sorry," said the Invisible Man, "if I cannot tell you all tonight. But I am worn out. I have made a discovery. I meant to keep it to myself. I can't. I must have a partner. We can do such things—but tomorrow. Now, Kemp, I feel as though I must sleep or perish."

"Then goodnight," said Kemp, and shook an invisible hand. He walked to the door. Suddenly the dressing-gown came quickly towards him. "Understand me!" said the gown. "No attempts to capture me! Or—"

Kemp's face changed a little. "I thought I gave you my word," he said.

Kemp closed the door softly behind him, and the key was turned upon him forthwith. Kemp slapped his brow with his hand. "Am I dreaming? Barred out of my own bedroom, by a flagrant absurdity!" He shook his head hopelessly, turned, and went downstairs.

He went into his little consulting room and lit the gas there. "Ah!" he said, and caught up the *St. James' Gazette*. "Now we shall get at the truth." He rent the paper open; a couple of columns confronted him. ENTIRE VILLAGE IN SUSSEX GOES MAD was the heading. RAN THROUGH THE STREETS STRIKING RIGHT AND LEFT. JAFFERS INSENSIBLE. MR. HUXTER IN GREAT PAIN. WOMEN ILL WITH TERROR! WINDOWS SMASHED.

"Good Heavens!" said Kemp, reading eagerly an incredulous account of the events in Iping the previous afternoon. He sat down abruptly on the surgical couch. "He's not only invisible," he said, "but he's mad! Homicidal! And where does the tramp come in?"

He was altogether too excited to sleep. He gave the servants instructions to lay breakfast

TERROR STORY FROM IPING!

WHOLE TOWN IN SUSSEX PANICS!

INVISIBLE STRIKES

for two in the study—and then to confine themselves to the ground floor. Then he continued to pace until the morning's paper came. That had much to say and little to tell, beyond the confirmation of the evening before and an account of another remarkable tale from Port Burdock. This gave Kemp the essence of the happenings at the Jolly Cricketers, and the name of Marvel. But there was nothing to throw light on the connection between the Invisible Man and the tramp; for Mr. Marvel had supplied no information about the books, or the money with which he was lined.

"It reads like rage growing to mania!" Kemp said, "The things he may do! And he's upstairs free as the air. What on earth ought I to do? Would it be a breach of faith if—? No."

He went to his desk and wrote a note. Then he took an envelope and addressed it to COLONEL ADYE, PORT BURDOCK.

The Invisible Man awoke even as Kemp was doing this. Kemp heard his feet rush suddenly across the bedroom overhead, then a chair was flung over and the washstand tumbler smashed. Kemp hurried upstairs and rapped eagerly. "What's the matter?" asked Kemp, when the Invisible Man admitted him.

"Fit of temper," said the Invisible Man. "Forgot this arm; and it's sore."

"You're rather liable to that sort of thing."

"I am."

"All the facts are out about you," said Kemp, "all that happened in Iping, and down the hill. But no one knows you are here."

The Invisible Man swore.

"There's breakfast upstairs," said Kemp. He led the way up the stairs to the belvedere.

"Before we can do anything else," said Kemp, "I must understand more about this invisibility of yours." He had sat down, after a nervous glance out of the window. He looked across to where Griffin sat at the table—a headless, handless dressing gown, wiping unseen lips on a miraculously held serviette.

"It's simple enough," said Griffin.

"No doubt, to you, but—" Kemp laughed.

"Well, yes; to me it seemed wonderful at first, no doubt. I came on the stuff first after I left London. You know I dropped medicine and took up physics? Light fascinated me. I found a general principle of pigments and refraction—a geometrical expression involving four dimensions. In the books—the books that tramp has hidden—there are marvels, miracles! It was a method by which it would be possible, without changing any other property of matter, to lower the refractive index of a substance, solid or liquid, to that of air."

"But personal invisibility is a far cry," said Kemp.

"Precisely," said Griffin. "But consider: visibility depends on the action of the visible bodies on light. A body absorbs light, or it reflects or refracts it. If it neither reflects nor refracts nor absorbs light, it cannot of itself be visible.

"And all that I had in mind after I left London—six years ago. But I had to work under frightful disadvantages. Oliver, my professor, was a scientific bounder, a journalist by instinct, a thief of ideas! I simply would not publish, and let him share my credit. I told no living soul, because I meant to flash my work upon the world with crushing effect—to become famous at a blow. And suddenly I made a discovery in physiology."

The Invisible Man rose and began pacing the little study. "I remember that night. It came suddenly, splendid and complete into my mind. One could make a tissue transparent! One could make it invisible! It was overwhelming.

"To do this would be to transcend magic. And I beheld, unclouded by doubt, a magnificent vision of all that invisibility might mean to a man—the mystery, the power, the freedom. Drawbacks I saw none. And I, a poverty-struck, hemmed-in demonstrator, teaching fools in a provincial college, might suddenly become—this. I worked three years, and every mountain of difficulty I toiled over showed another from its summit. The infinite details!

"I had left the college and had taken a room in London, a large unfurnished room in an ill-managed lodging house. The work was going on steadily, drawing near an end. And now there was scarcely a difficulty left, beyond the planning of details.

"I will tell you, Kemp, sooner or later, all the complicated processes. They are written in cypher in those books that tramp has hidden. We must hunt him down. We must get those books again. But the essential phase was to place the object whose refractive index was to be lowered between two radiating centres of a sort of ethereal vibration. I needed two little dynamos, and these I worked with a cheap gas engine. My first experiment was with a bit of white wool fabric. I was the strangest thing in

the world to see it in the flicker of the flashes soft and white, and then to watch it fade like a wreath of smoke and vanish.

"Then I heard a miaow behind me, and turning, saw a lean white cat outside. I went to the window, opened it, and called softly. She came in, purring—the poor beast was starving—and I gave her some milk. After that she went smelling round the room, evidently with the idea of making herself at home."

"And you processed her?"

"I processed her. I gave the beast opium, and put her on the apparatus. And after all the rest had faded, there remained two little ghosts of her eyes. She was bandaged and clamped, of course, so I had her safe; but she woke while she was still misty, and miaowed dismally, and someone came knocking. It was an old woman from downstairs, who suspected me of vivisecting. I whipped out some chloroform and applied it to the cat, then answered the door. 'Did I hear a cat?' she asked. 'My cat?' 'Not here,' said I, very politely. She was a little doubtful and tried to peer past me into the room. She had to be satisfied at last and went away."

"How long did it take?" asked Kemp.

"Three or four hours. The bones and sinews and the fat were the last to go, and the tips of the coloured hairs. And, as I say, the back part of the eye, tough iridescent stuff it is, wouldn't go at all.

"It was night long before the business was over, and nothing was to be seen but the dim eyes and the claws. I stopped the engine, felt for the beast, which was still insensible, and then, being tired, left it sleeping and went to bed. About two, the cat began miaowing. I remember the shock I had when striking a light—there were just the eyes shining green—and nothing round them. It wouldn't be quiet, it just sat and miaowed at the door. At last I opened the window and made a bustle. I suppose it went out at last. I never saw any more of it."

"You don't mean to say there's an invisible cat at large!" said Kemp.

"If it hasn't been killed," said the Invisible Man. "It was alive four days after, I know, and down a street grating; because I saw a crowd trying to see whence the miaowing came.

"I was surprised to find, now that my prize was within my grasp, how inconclusive its attainment seemed. All I could think clearly was that the thing had to be carried through. And soon, for the money I had was almost exhausted. I went to sleep that night thinking of all the fantastic advantages an invisible man would have in the world.

"When I awoke there was someone rapping at the door. It was my landlord with threats and inquiries. I had been tormenting a cat in the night he was sure. The laws of this country against vivisection were very severe—he might be liable. I denied the cat. What was I doing? Why was I always alone and secretive? Was it legal? Was it dangerous? His had always been a most respectable house—

"Suddenly my temper gave way. I told him to get out. He began to protest, to jabber of his right of entry. In a moment I had him by the collar and he went spinning out into the passage. I slammed and locked the door and sat down quivering.

"He made a fuss outside, and after a time he went away.

"But this brought matters to a crisis. I did not know what he would do. To move to fresh apartments would have meant delay, and I could not afford that. Vanish! It was irresistible.

"I hurried out with my three books of notes—the tramp has them now—and directed them from the nearest Post Office to a house of call for letters and parcels.

"It was all done that night. While I was still sitting under the sickly, drowsy influence of the drugs that decolourise blood, there came a repeated knocking at the door. In a fit of irritation I rose and went and flung the door wide open. It was my landlord, with a notice of ejectment or something. He held it out to me, saw something odd about my hands, I expect, and lifted his eyes to my face.

"For a moment he gaped. Then he gave an inarticulate cry, dropped candle and writ together, and went blundering down the dark passage to the stairs. I shut the door, locked it, and went to the looking glass. My face was white — like stone.

"It was horrible. I had not expected the suffering. My skin was presently afire. I became insensible and woke languid in the darkness.

"The pain had passed. I shall never forget that dawn, and the strange horror of seeing that my hands had become as clouded glass, and watching them grow clearer and thinner as the day went by, until at last I could see the room through them, though I closed my transparent eyelids. My limbs became glassy, the bones and arteries faded, and the little white nerves went last. At last only the dead tips of the finger-nails remained, pallid and white.

"I struggled up. I was weak and very hungry. I went and stared at nothing in my shaving glass, save where an attenuated pigment still remained behind the retina of my eyes, fainter than mist. It was only by a frantic effort of will that I dragged myself back to the apparatus and completed the process.

"I slept during the forenoon, and about midday I was awakened again by a knocking. Heavy blows began to rain upon the door. I stepped out of the window, lowered the sash, and sat down to watch events. They split a panel, and in another moment they stood in the open doorway. It was the landlord and his two step-sons. Behind them fluttered the old hag from downstairs. You may imagine their astonishment on finding the room empty. One of the younger men rushed to the window at once and stared out. His thick-lipped face came a foot from my face. He stared right through me.

"The old man agreed with the old lady that I was a vivisectionist. The sons protested that I was an electrician, and appealed to the dynamos and radiators.

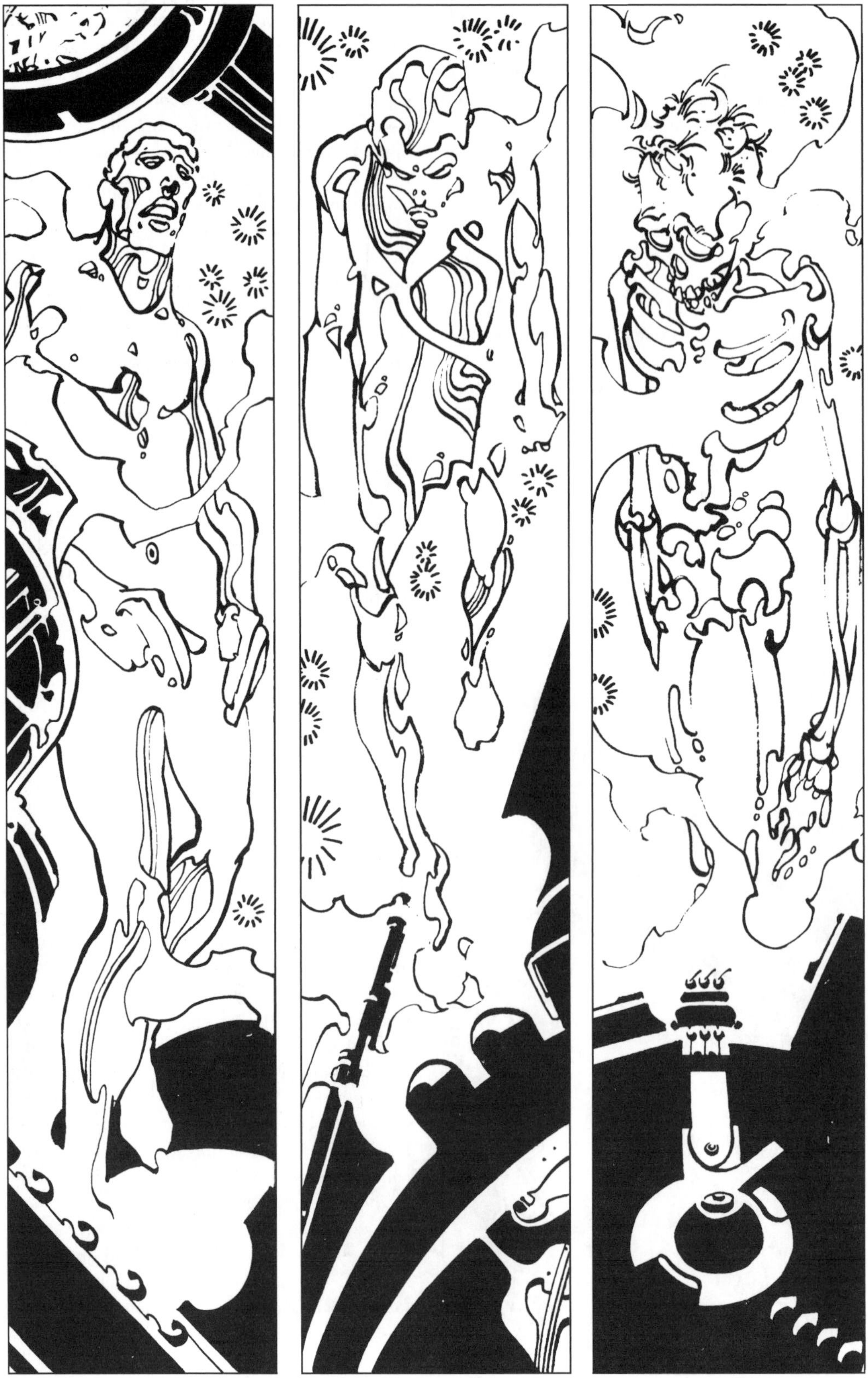

"I went into one of the sitting-rooms and waited until they came down. Then I slipped up again with a box of matches, fired a heap of paper and rubbish, led the gas to the affair by means of a rubber tube, and waving a farewell to the room left it for the last time."

"You fired the house!" cried Kemp.

"Fired the house. It was the only way to cover my trail. I went out into the street. My head was already teeming with plans of all the wonderful things I had now impunity to do."

My mood, I say, was one of exaltation. I experienced a wild impulse to startle people, to fling people's hats astray, and generally revel in my extraordinary advantage.

"I tried to get into the stream of people, but they were too thick for me, and in a moment my heels were being trodden upon. I took to the gutter, the roughness of which I found painful to my feet, and forthwith the shaft of a crawling hansom dug me forcibly under the shoulder blade. I staggered out of the way of the cab, avoided a perambulator by a convulsive movement, and found myself behind the hansom. A happy thought saved me, and as this drove slowly along I followed in its immediate wake, trembling and astonished at the turn of my adventure. And not only trembling, but shivering. It was a bright day in January and I was stark naked and the thin slime of mud that covered the road was freezing. Foolish as it seems to me now, I had not reckoned that, transparent or not, I was still amenable to the weather and all its consequences.

"I made off up the roadway, intending to strike north and so get into the quiet district. I was chilled, and the strangeness of my situation unnerved me. At the northward corner of Bloomsbury Square a little white dog made for me, nose down. The brute began barking and leaping, showing only too plainly that he was aware of me. I crossed Russell Street and ran up the steps of a house facing the Museum railings. Happily the dog hesitated, and turned tail, running back to the Square again.

"I did not at first notice two urchins stopping at the railings by me. 'See 'em,' said one. 'See what?' said the other. 'Why—them footmarks—bare. Like what you makes in mud.'

"'Looky there, Ted,' quoth the younger of the detectives, and pointed straight to my feet.

I looked down and saw at once the suggestion of their outline sketched in splashes of mud.

"'It's like the ghost of a foot, ain't it?' said the elder. He advanced with outstretched hand. A man pulled up short to see what he was catching, and then a girl. In another moment he would have touched me. With a rapid movement I swung myself over into the portico of the next house. But the smaller boy was sharp-eyed enough to follow the movement and before I was down the steps he was shouting that the feet had gone over the wall.

"In another moment I was rushing round Russell Square, with six or seven astonished people following my footmarks. At last I had a breathing space and rubbed my feet clean with my hands, and so got away altogether. The last I saw of the chase was a little group of a dozen people studying a slowly drying footprint.

"I went on through less frequented roads. My feet hurt exceedingly. Once or twice accidental collisions occurred and I left people amazed, with unaccountable curses ringing in their ears. Every dog that came in sight was a terror to me.

The Invisible Man paused and thought. Kemp glanced nervously out of the window. "Yes?" he said. "Go on."

"So last January, with the beginning of a snowstorm in the air about me—and if it settled on me it would betray me!—weary, cold and inexpressibly wretched, I began this new life to which I am committed. I had no refuge, no appliances, no being in the world in whom I could confide. My sole object was to get shelter; then I might hope to plan. But even to me, an Invisible Man, the London houses stood latched and bolted impregnably.

"Then I remembered that some theatrical costumiers had shops in that district. Every crossing was a danger, every pedestrian a thing to watch alertly. At last I reached the object of my quest, a dirty little shop in a byway near Drury Lane with a window full of tinsel robes, sham jewels, wigs, and theatrical photographs. I peered through the window and, seeing no one within, entered. The opening of the door set a bell ringing. For a minute or so no one came. Then I heard heavy feet striding across a room, and a man entered. He stared about with an expression of expectation. This gave way to

anger as he saw the shop empty. 'Damn the boys!' he said. He had left the house door open and I slipped into the inner room.

"It was poorly furnished and with a number of masks in the corner. On the table was his belated breakfast, and it was a confoundedly exasperating thing for me to have to stand watching while he resumed his meal. Three doors opened into the little room, but they were all shut. I could not get out while he was there, I could scarcely move because of his alertness. Twice I strangled a sneeze just in time.

"At last he made an end to his eating and putting his crockery on a tray he took the whole lot of things after him. His burden prevented his shutting the door behind him, and I went upstairs and sat in his chair by the fire. It was burning low, and scarcely thinking, I put on a little coal. The noise of this brought him up at once. He peered about the room and was within an ace of touching me. Even after that examination, he scarcely seemed satisfied. He stopped in the doorway and took a final inspection before he went down.

"I waited in the little parlour for an age, and at last he came and opened the upstairs door. I just managed to get by him.

"On the staircase he stopped suddenly, so that I very nearly blundered into him. He stood looking back right into my face and listening. He was becoming aware of the faint sounds of my movements about him. The man must have had diabolically acute hearing. He suddenly flashed into rage. 'If there's any one in this house,' he cried with an oath, and left the threat unfinished. He went pugnaciously downstairs.

"I resolved to explore the house, and spent some time in doing so as noiselessly as possible. In one room next to his I found a lot of old clothes. I began routing among these, and in my eagerness forgot again the evident sharpness of his ears. I heard a stealthy footstep and, looking up just in time, saw him peering in at the tumbled heap and holding an old-fashioned revolver. I stood perfectly still while he stared about open-mouthed and suspicious.

"Then the infernal brute started going all over the house, and locking door after door and pocketing the keys. And so I made no more ado, but knocked him on the head."

"Knocked him on the head!" exclaimed Kemp.

"Yes, as he was going downstairs. Hit him from behind with a stool that stood on the landing. He went downstairs like a bag of old boots."

"But—! The common conventions of humanity—"

"Are all very well for common people. But the point was, I had to get out of that house without his seeing me. I couldn't think of any other way of doing it."

Kemp's face grew a trifle hard. He was about to speak and checked himself. "I suppose, after all," he said with a sudden change of manner, "the thing had to be done. You were in a fix. But still—"

"Of course I was in a fix. And he made me wild too—hunting me about the house, fooling about with his revolver, locking and unlocking doors. He was simply exasperating.

"I was hungry. Downstairs I found a loaf and some cheese. Then I went up past the shopkeeper—he was lying quite still—to the room containing the clothes. I chose a mask, slightly grotesque but not more so than many human beings, dark glasses, whiskers, and a wig. The hunchback's boots were rather a loose fit and sufficed. In a desk in the shop were three sovereigns and about thirty shillings' worth of silver, and in a locked cupboard I burst in the inner room were eight pounds in gold. I could go forth into the world again, equipped.

"I spent some minutes screwing up my courage and then unlocked the shop door and marched out into the street. No one appeared to notice me. I thought my troubles were over. Whatever I did, whatever the consequences might be, was nothing to me. I had merely to fling aside my garments and vanish. No person could hold me. I could take my money where I found it. I decided to treat myself to a sumptuous feast, and then put up at a good hotel, and accumulate a new outfit of property. I went into a place and was already ordering a lunch, when it occurred to me that I could not eat unless I exposed my invisible face. I went out exasperated. At last, faint with the desire for food, I went into another place and demanded a private room. 'I am disfigured,' I said. 'Badly.' They looked at me curiously, but of course it was not their affair—and so at last I got my lunch.

"Before I made this mad experiment I had dreamt of a thousand advantages. That afternoon it seemed all disappointment. No doubt invisibility made it possible to get things, but it made it impossible to enjoy them when they are got. And for this I had become a wrapped-up mystery, a swathed and bandaged caricature of a man!"

"But how did you get to Iping?" said Kemp, anxious to keep his guest talking.

"I went there to work. I had one hope. Of restoring what I have done. When I have done all I mean to do invisibly."

"At the end," said Kemp, "when they found you out, you rather—to judge by the papers—"

"Did I kill that fool of a constable?"

"No," said Kemp. "He's expected to recover."

"That's his luck, then. I clean lost my temper, the fools! Why couldn't they leave me alone? By Heaven, Kemp, you don't know what rage is! To have worked for years, to have planned and plotted, and then to get some fumbling purblind idiot messing across your course! If I have much more of it, I shall go wild—I shall start mowing 'em."

"No doubt it's exasperating," said Kemp, dryly. "But now," with a glance out the window, "what are we to do?"

He moved nearer his guest as he spoke to prevent the possibility of a glimpse of the three men advancing up the road.

"I was going to clear out of the country. But I have altered that plan since seeing you. I thought it would be wise to make for the South. I was using that tramp as a money box and luggage carrier, until I decided how to get my books and things sent to meet me."

"That's clear."

"And then the filthy brute tried to rob me! He has hidden my books, Kemp. If I can lay my hands on him!"

"He's in the town police station, locked up, by his own request, in the strongest cell in the place."

"We must get those books; those books are vital."

"Certainly," said Kemp, a little nervously, hearing footsteps outside. "That won't be difficult if he doesn't know they're for you."

"Blundering into your house, Kemp," Griffin said, "changes all my plans. For you are a man that can understand. In spite of all that has happened, in spite of the loss of my books, there still remain great possibilities—"

"You have told no one I am here?" he asked abruptly.

"Not a soul."

"I made a mistake, Kemp, in carrying this thing through alone. I have wasted strength, time, opportunities. How little a man can do alone! To rob a little, to hurt a little, and there is the end. I must have a confederate. With a confederate, with food and rest—a thousand things are possible.

"We have to consider all that invisibility means, all that it does not mean. It means little advantage for eavesdropping and so forth—one makes sounds. It's of little help in housebreaking and so forth. Once you've caught me you could easily imprison me. But on the other hand I am hard to catch. This invisibility, in fact, is only good in two cases: it's useful in getting away, it's useful in approaching. It's particularly useful, therefore, in killing. I can walk round a man, choose my point, strike as I like. Dodge as I like. Escape as I like. And it is killing we must do, Kemp."

"Why killing?"

"Not wanton killing but a judicious slaying. The point is they know there is an Invisible Man. And that Invisible Man must now establish a reign of terror. He must take some town like your Burdock and dominate it. And all who disobey his orders he must kill, and kill all who would defend the disobedient."

"It seems to me," said Kemp, no longer listening to Griffin but to the sound of his front door opening, "that your confederate would be in a difficult position."

"No one would know he was a confederate," said the Invisible Man, eagerly. And then suddenly, "Hush! What's that downstairs?"

"Nothing," said Kemp, and suddenly began to speak loud and fast. "I don't agree to this, Griffin," he said. "Publish your results; take the world into your confidence—"

The Invisible Man interrupted Kemp. "There are footsteps coming upstairs," he said in a low voice.

"Nonsense," said Kemp.

"Let me see," said the Invisible Man, and advanced, arm extended, to the door.

Kemp moved to intercept him. "Traitor!" cried Griffin, and suddenly the dressing gown opened, and he began to disrobe. Kemp flung the door open. With a quick movement Kemp thrust the Invisible Man back, sprang aside, and slammed the door. He tried to grip the door handle with both hands. He stood lugging for a moment. Then the door was jerked a foot wide, and the dressing-gown came wedging itself into the opening. His throat was gripped by invisible fingers, and he left his hold on the handle to defend himself. He was forced back, tripped and pitched heavily into the corner of the landing. The empty dressing gown was flung on the top of him.

Halfway up the staircase was Colonel Adye, the recipient of Kemp's letter, the chief of the Burdock police. He was staring aghast at the sudden appearance of Kemp, followed by the extraordinary sight of clothing tossing empty in the air. He saw Kemp felled, and struggling to his feet. He saw him rush forward, and go down again, felled like an ox.

Then suddenly he was struck violently. By nothing! A vast weight leapt upon him, and he was hurled headlong down the staircase, with a grip at his throat and a knee in his groin. An invisible foot trod on his back and a ghostly patter passed downstairs. He heard the two police officers in the hall shout and run, and the front door of the house slammed violently.

He rolled over and sat up staring. He saw, staggering down the staircase, Kemp, his lip bleeding, holding a dressing gown in his arms.

"My God!" cried Kemp, "the game's up! He's gone!"

For a space Kemp was too inarticulate to make Adye understand what had happened. But presently Adye began to grasp the situation. "He's mad," said Kemp; "inhuman. I have listened to such a story of brutal self-seeking! He will kill unless we can prevent him."

"He must be caught," said Adye. "That is certain."

"You must begin at once." cried Kemp. "You must prevent his leaving this district, Once he gets away he may go through the countryside as he wills, killing and maiming. He dreams of a reign of terror! You must set a watch on trains and roads and shipping. The only thing that may keep him here is the thought of recovering some books of notes he counts of value. There is a man in your police station—Marvel."

"I know," said Adye, "Those books —"

"And you must prevent him from eating or sleeping; day and night the country must be astir for him. Food must be locked up and secured so that he will have to break his way to it. Houses everywhere must be barred against him. Heaven send us cold nights and rain! The whole countryside must begin hunting and keep hunting. I tell you, Adye, unless he is pinned and secured, it is frightful to think of the things that may happen."

In another moment Adye was leading the way downstairs. They found the policemen standing outside staring at empty air. "He's got away, sir," said one.

"We must go to the central station at once," said Adye.

"Dogs," said Kemp. "Get dogs. They don't see him, but they wind him."

"Good," said Adye. "What else?"

"And on the roads," Kemp hesitated.

"Yes?" said Adye.

"Powdered glass," said Kemp. "It's cruel, I know. But think of what he may do! He has cut himself off from his kind. His blood be upon his own head."

In a great circle of twenty miles round Port Burdock, armed men were presently setting out in groups of three and four, with dogs, to beat the roads and fields.

Mounted policemen rode along the country lanes, warning the people to lock their houses and keep indoors. So swift and decided was the action of the authorities that before nightfall an area of several hundred square miles was in a stringent state of siege. And before nightfall, too, a thrill of horror went through the whole watching nervous countryside. Going from whispering mouth to mouth over the length and breadth of the county passed the story of the murder of Mr. Wicksteed.

Wicksteed was a man of inoffensive habits and appearance, the very last person in the world to provoke such a terrible antagonist. Against him it would seem the Invisible Man used an iron rod dragged from a broken fence. He stopped this quiet man, going home to his midday meal, attacked him, beat down his feeble defenses, and smashed his head to a jelly.

After the murder of Mr. Wicksteed, the Invisible Man would seem to have struck towards the downland. There is a story of a voice heard about sunset by a couple of men near Fern Bottom. It was wailing and laughing, sobbing and groaning. It drove up across the middle of a clover field and died away towards the hills. In the night, he must have eaten and slept; for in the morning he was himself again, powerful, angry, and malignant, prepared for his great struggle against the world.

The next day, Kemp received a strange missive, written in pencil on a greasy sheet of paper.

YOU HAVE BEEN AMAZINGLY ENERGETIC AND CLEVER, THOUGH WHAT YOU STAND TO GAIN BY IT I CANNOT IMAGINE. FOR A WHOLE DAY YOU HAVE CHASED ME; YOU HAVE TRIED TO ROB ME OF A NIGHT'S REST. BUT I HAVE HAD FOOD IN SPITE OF YOU, I HAVE SLEPT IN SPITE OF YOU, AND THE GAME IS ONLY BEGINNING. THIS ANNOUNCES THE FIRST DAY OF THE TERROR. PORT BURDOCK IS NO LONGER UNDER THE QUEEN. TELL YOUR COLONEL OF POLICE, AND THE REST OF THEM; IT IS UNDER ME— THE TERROR! THIS IS DAY ONE OF YEAR ONE OF THE NEW EPOCH—THE EPOCH OF THE

INVISIBLE MAN. THE FIRST DAY THERE WILL BE ONE EXECUTION FOR THE SAKE OF EXAMPLE—A MAN NAMED KEMP. HE MAY LOCK HIMSELF AWAY, GET GUARDS ABOUT HIM; THE UNSEEN DEATH IS COMING. HELP HIM NOT, MY PEOPLE, LEST DEATH FALL UPON YOU ALSO. TODAY KEMP IS TO DIE.

Kemp read this letter twice. "It's no hoax," he said. "That's his voice! And he means it."

He got up, leaving his lunch unfinished—the letter had come by the one o'clock post—and went into his study. He rang for his housekeeper, and told her to go round the house at once and close all the shutters. From a drawer in his bedroom he took a revolver and put it into his pocket. He wrote a note to Colonel Adye and gave it to his servant to take, with explicit instructions as to her way of leaving the house. "There is no danger," he said, "to you." He then returned to his cooling lunch.

Finally he struck the table sharply. "We will have him!" he said; "and I am the bait. He will come too far."

He went up to the belvedere, carefully shutting every door after him. "It's a game," he said, "an odd game—but the chances are all for me, Mr. Griffin, in spite of your invisibility."

Presently he heard the front door bell ringing, and hurried downstairs. He unbolted and unlocked the door, put up the chain, and opened cautiously without showing himself. A familiar voice hailed him. It was Adye.

"Your servant's been assaulted, Kemp," he said round the door.

"What!" exclaimed Kemp.

"Had that note of yours taken away from her. Let me in."

Kemp released the chain, and Adye entered through as narrow an opening as possible. He stood in the hall as Kemp refastened the door. "Note was snatched out of her hand. Scared her horribly. She's down at the station. He's close here. What was it about?"

"Look here!" said Kemp, and led the way into his study. He handed Adye the Invisible Man's letter. Adye read it and whistled softly. "And you—?" said Adye.

"Proposed a trap—like a fool," said Kemp, "and sent my proposal out by a maid servant. To him."

A resounding smash of glass came from upstairs. Adye had a glimpse of the revolver half out of Kemp's pocket. When they reached the study they found the windows smashed, the room littered with glass, and a big flint on the writing table.

"What's this for?" said Adye.

"It's a beginning," said Kemp.

A smash, and then the whack of boards hit hard came from downstairs. "Confound him!" said Kemp. "He's going to do all the house."

Another window proclaimed its destruction. "Let me have a stick or something, said Adye, "and I'll go down to the station and get the bloodhounds. That ought to settle him!"

Another window went the way of its fellows. "You haven't a revolver?" asked Adye.

Kemp hesitated. "I haven't one—at least to spare."

"I'll bring it back," said Adye, "you'll be safe here." Kemp handed him the weapon.

As they stood hesitating in the hall, they heard one of the first floor bedroom windows crash. Kemp went to the door and slipped the bolts as silently as possible. His face was pale. "You must step straight out," said Kemp. In another moment Adye was on the doorstep and the bolts were dropping back into the staples. He hesitated for a moment, feeling more comfortable with his back against the door. Then he marched down the steps. crossed the lawn and approached the gate. A little breeze seemed to ripple over the grass. Something moved near him. "Stop," said a voice. Adye stopped dead and his hand tightened on the revolver.

"Oblige me by going back to the house," said the voice.

"Where I go," Adye said slowly, "is my own business." The words were still on his lips, when an arm came round his neck, his back felt a knee, and he was sprawling backward. He drew clumsily and fired, and in another moment he was struck in the mouth and the revolver wrested from his grip. He made a vain clutch at a slippery limb and fell back.

The voice laughed. "I'd kill you now if it wasn't the waste of a bullet," it said. Adye saw the revolver in mid-air, covering him.

"Well?" said Adaye, sitting up.

"Get up," said the voice, and then fiercely, "Don't try any games. Remember I can see your face if you can't see mine. You've got to go back to the house."

"He won't let me in," said Adye.

"That's a pity," said the Invisible Man. "I've got no quarrel with you."

Adye turned towards the house, walking slowly. Kemp watched him from the study window. The revolver was a little dark object following Adye. Then things happened very quickly. Adye leapt backwards, swung round, clutched at this little object, missed it, threw up his hands and fell forward on his face, leaving a little puff of blue in the air. Kemp did not hear the sound of the shot. Adye writhed, raised himself on one arm, fell forward, and lay still.

Then came a ringing and knocking at the front door, that grew tumultuous. This was followed by a silence. Kemp armed himself with his bedroom poker, and went to examine the fastenings of the ground floor windows again. He returned to the belvedere. Adye lay motionless over the edge of the gravel just as he had fallen. Coming along the road were the housemaid and two policemen.

There was a smash from below. He hesitated and went downstairs again. Suddenly the house resounded with heavy blows and the splintering of wood. He turned the key and opened the kitchen door. As he did so, the shutters came flying inward. The shutters had been driven in with an axe, and now the axe was descending in sweeping blows upon the window frame and the iron bars defending it. He saw the revolver lying on the path outside, and then the little weapon sprang into the air. He dodged back. The revolver cracked just too late, and a splinter from the edge of the closing door flashed over his head. He slammed and locked the door, and as he stood outside he heard Griffin shouting and laughing. Then the blows of the axe, with their splitting and smashing accompaniments, were resumed.

Kemp stood in the passage trying to think. In a moment the Invisible Man would be in the kitchen. This door would not keep him a moment, and then—

A ringing came at the front door. It would be the policemen. He ran into the hall, put up the chain, and drew the bolts. The three people blundered into the house in a heap, and Kemp slammed the door again.

"The Invisible Man!" said Kemp. "He has a revolver, with two shots left. He's killed Adye."

"What's that smashing?" asked one of the policemen.

"He's in the kitchen—or will be. He has found an axe—"

"This way," cried Kemp, and bundled the policemen into the dining room doorway.

Kemp rushed to the fender and handed a poker to each policeman. He suddenly flung himself backward.

"Whup!" said one policeman, ducked, and caught the axe on his poker. The pistol snapped its penultimate shot as the second policeman brought his poker down on the little weapon and sent it rattling to the floor.

The axe receded into the passage, and fell to a position about two feet from the ground. They could hear the Invisible Man breathing. "Stand away, you two," he said. "I want that man Kemp."

"We want you," said the first policeman, making a quick step forward and wiping with his poker at the voice. Then, as the policeman staggered with the swing of the blow he had aimed, the Invisible Man countered with the axe, the helmet crumpled like paper, and the blow sent the man spinning to the floor at the head of the stairs. But the second policeman, aiming behind the axe with his poker, hit something soft that snapped. There was a sharp exclamation of pain and the axe fell to the ground. The policeman wiped again at vacancy and hit nothing. Then he stood, listening intent for the slightest movement.

He heard the dining room window open, and a quick rush of feet within. His companion sat up with blood running down between his eye and ear. "Where is he?" asked the man on the floor.

"Don't know. I've hit him. He's somewhere in the hall. Unless he's slipped past you. Doctor Kemp—sir."

Pause.

"Doctor Kemp," cried the policeman again.

The dining room window was wide open, and neither housemaid nor Kemp was to be seen.

Emerging into the hill-road, Kemp took the downward direction. He ran with wide strides, and wherever a patch of rough ground intervened, wherever there came a patch of raw flints, or a bit of broken glass shone dazzling, he crossed it and left the bare invisible feet that followed to take what line they would.

The people below were staring at him, one or two were running, and his breath was beginning to saw in his throat. In another moment he had passed the door of the Jolly Cricketers, and was in the end of the street, with human beings about him.

His pace broke a little, then he heard the swift pad of his pursuer, and leapt forward again. "The Invisible Man!" he cried, and placed a group between him and the chase. He turned into a little side street, and then made for the mouth of an alley that ran back into Hill Street again. Immediately he became aware of a tumultuous vociferation and running people.

He glanced up the street towards the hill. Hardly a dozen yards off ran a huge navvy, cursing and slashing viciously with a spade, and hard behind him came the tram conductor with his fists clenched. Up the street others followed these two, striking and shouting. Down towards the town, men and women were running. "Spread out!" cried someone. Kemp suddenly grasped the altered condition of the chase. He stopped and looked round, panting. "He's close here!" he cried. "Form a line across—"

"Aha!" shouted a voice.

He was hit hard under the ear, and went reeling, trying to face round towards his unseen antagonist. He just managed to keep his feet, and he struck a vain counter in the air. Then he was hit again under the jaw, and sprawled headlong on the ground. In another moment eager hands gripped his throat. He grasped the wrists, then heard a cry of pain from his assailant, as the spade of the navvy came whirling through the air above him, and struck something with a dull thud. He felt a drop of moisture on his face. The grip at his throat suddenly relaxed, and with a convulsive effort Kemp loosed himself, grasped a limp shoulder, and rolled uppermost. He gripped the unseen elbows near the ground. "I've got him!" screamed Kemp. "He's down! Hold his feet!"

In another second there was a simultaneous rush upon the struggle. With a mighty

effort the Invisible Man threw off a couple of his antagonists and rose to his knees. Kemp clung to him in front like a hound to a stag, and a dozen hands gripped, clutched, and tore at the unseen. The tram conductor suddenly got the neck and shoulders and lugged him back.

Down went the heap of struggling men again and rolled over. There was some savage kicking. Then suddenly a wild scream of "Mercy! Mercy!" that died down swiftly to a sound like choking.

"Get back, you fools!" cried Kemp. "He's hurt, I tell you. Stand back!"

There was a brief struggle to clear a space, and then the circle of eager eyes saw the doctor kneeling, as it seemed, fifteen inches in the air, and holding invisible arms to the ground. Behind him a constable gripped invisible ankles.

"Don't you leave go of en," cried the big navvy, holding a bloodstained spade; "he's shamming."

"He's not shamming," said the doctor, cautiously raising his knee. His face was bruised and he spoke thickly because of a bleeding lip. Kemp felt about, his hand seeming to pass through empty air. "The mouth's all wet. He's not breathing," he said, and then, "I can't feel his heart."

He stood up abruptly and then knelt down on the ground by the side of the thing unseen. There was a pushing and shuffling, a sound of heavy feet as fresh people turned up to increase the pressure of the crowd.

Suddenly an old woman, peering under the arm of the big navvy, screamed sharply. "Looky there!" she said, and thrust out a wrinkled finger.

And looking where she pointed, everyone saw, faint and transparent as though it was made of glass, so that veins and arteries and bones and nerves could be distinguished, the outline of a hand, limp and prone. It grew clouded and opaque even as they stared.

"Hullo!" cried the constable. "Here's his feet a-showing!"

And so, slowly, beginning at his hands and feet and creeping along his limbs to the vital centres of his body, that strange change continued. It was like the slow spreading of a poison. First came the little white nerves, a hazy grey sketch of a limb, then the glassy bones and intricate arteries, then the flesh and skin, first a faint fogginess and then growing rapidly dense and opaque. Presently they could see his crushed chest and the dim outline of his drawn and battered features.

When at last the crowd made way for Kemp to stand erect, there lay, naked and pitiful on the ground, the bruised and broken body of a young man. His hands were clenched, his eyes wide open, and his expression was one of anger and dismay.

"Cover his face!" said a man. "For Gawd's sake, cover that face!" Children, pushing forward through the crowd, were suddenly twisted around and sent packing off again.

Someone brought a sheet from the Jolly Cricketers; and having covered him, they carried him into that house.

So ends the story of the strange and evil experiment of the Invisible Man. And if you would learn more you must go to a little inn near Port Stowe and talk to the landlord. The sign of the inn is an empty board save for a hat and boots, and the name is the title of this story. Drink generously, and the landlord will tell you of how the lawyers tried to do him out of the treasure found upon him.

"When they found they couldn't prove whose money was which, I'm blessed," he says, "if they didn't try to make me out a blooming treasure trove! And then a gentleman gave me a guinea a night to tell the story at the Empire Music 'all—just tell 'em in my own words—"

And if you want to cut off the flow of his reminiscences abruptly, you can always do so by asking if there weren't three books in the story. He admits there were and proceeds to explain that everybody thinks he has 'em! But he hasn't. "The Invisible Man took 'em off to hide 'em when I cut and ran for Port Stowe. It's that Mr. Kemp put people on with the idea of my having 'em."

He is a bachelor man, and on Sunday mornings, while he is closed to the outer world, and every night after ten, he goes into his bar parlour bearing a glass of gin faintly tinged with water. Having placed this down, he locks the door and examines the blinds, and even looks under the table. And then, being satisfied of his solitude, he unlocks the cupboard and produces three volumes bound in brown leather, and places them solemnly in the middle of the table. The covers are weather-worn and tinged with an algal green—for once they sojourned in a ditch and some of the pages have been washed blank by dirty water. The landlord sits down in an armchair, fills a long clay pipe slowly, gloating over the books the while. Then he pulls one towards him and opens it, and begins to study it—turning over the leaves backwards and forwards.

Presently he leans back, and blinks through his smoke across the room at things invisible to other eyes. "Full of secrets," he says. "Wonderful secrets! Once I get the haul of them—Lord!

"I wouldn't do what he did; I'd just—well!" He pulls at his pipe.

So he lapses into a dream, the undying wonderful dream of his life. And though Kemp has fished unceasingly, and the police have questioned closely, no human being save the landlord knows those books are there, with the subtle secret of invisibility written therein. And none other will know of them until he dies.

THE MAN
Who Could Work
MIRACLES

adapted & illustrated by

DAN O'NEILL

Story by H.G. Wells

THE MAN WHO COULD WORK MIRACLES.. BY H.G. WELLS

IT IS DOUBTFUL WHETHER THE GIFT WAS INNATE.. IT CAME SUDDENLY.. UNTIL HE WAS THIRTY HE WAS A SCEPTIC, AND DID **NOT** BELIEVE IN MIRACULOUS POWERS.. HIS NAME WAS **GEORGE McWHIRTER FOTHERINGAY..** ADDICTED TO ASSERTIVE ARGUMENT, IT WAS WHILE ASSERTING THE **IMPOSSIBILITY** OF MIRACLES, HE HAD HIS FIRST INTIMATION OF HIS EXTRAORDINARY POWERS.

LOOKY HERE, MR. BEAMISH.. LET US CLEARLY UNDERSTAND WHAT A MIRACLE IS..

..SOMETHING CONTRARIWISE TO THE COURSE OF NATURE. DONE BY THE POWER OF WILL ..

..SO YOU SAY..

SOMETHING WHAT COULDN'T HAPPEN **WITHOUT** BEING SPECIALLY WILLED.. FOR INSTANCE.. HERE WOULD BE A MIRACLE.. THAT **LAMP**..IN THE NATURAL COURSE OF NATURE COULDN'T BURN LIKE THAT UPSY-DOWN..?

..NO, IT COULDN'T..

..THEN HERE COMES SOMEONE.. ME..COLLECTING **ALL** MY WILL.. AND SAYS TO THAT LAMP.. **TURN UPSY-DOWN AND GO ON BURNING STEADY, AND..**

HULLO!

41

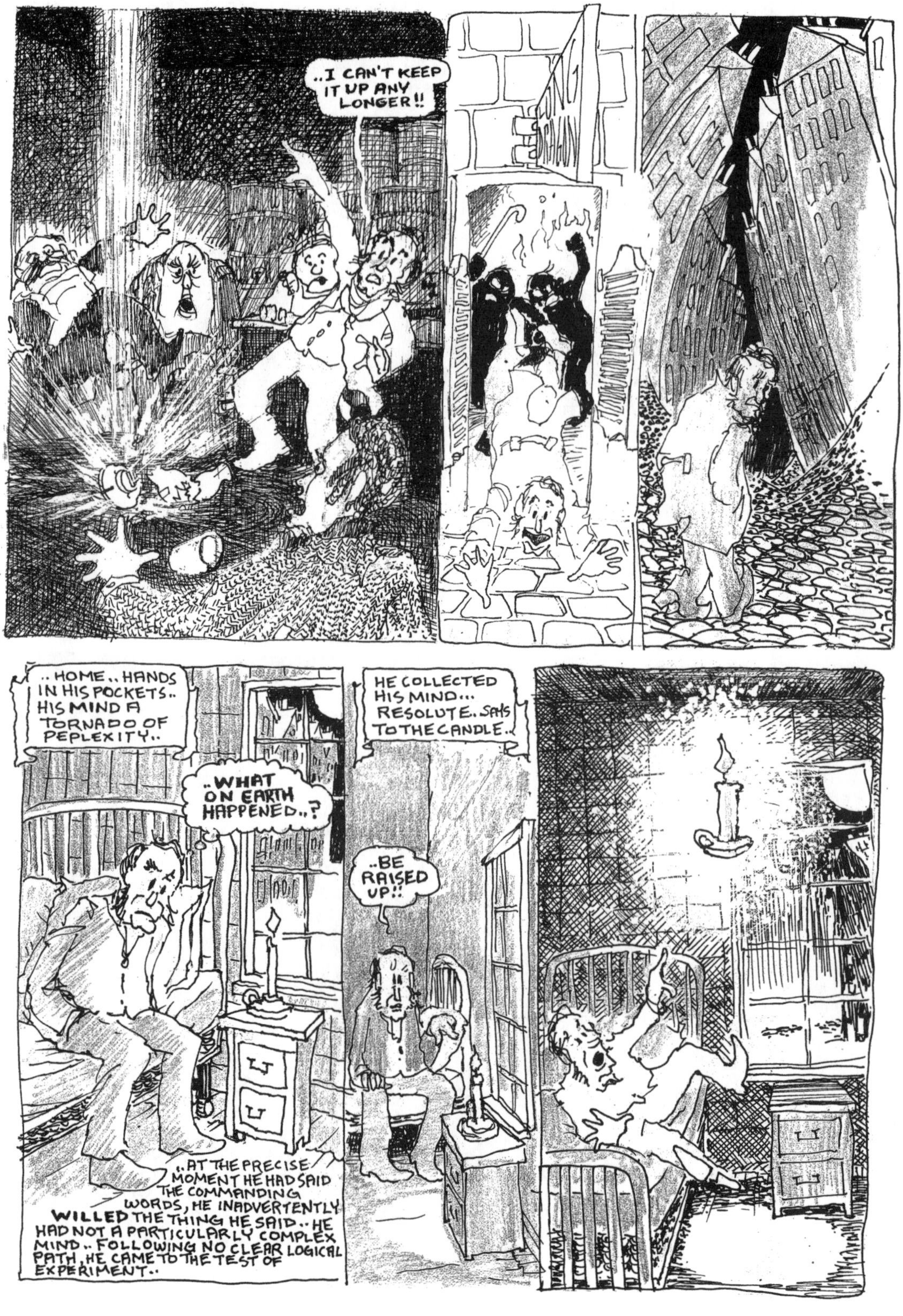
..I CAN'T KEEP IT UP ANY LONGER!!
..HOME.. HANDS IN HIS POCKETS.. HIS MIND A TORNADO OF PEPLEXITY..
..WHAT ON EARTH HAPPENED..?
..AT THE PRECISE MOMENT HE HAD SAID THE COMMANDING WORDS, HE INADVERTENTLY WILLED THE THING HE SAID.. HE HAD NOT A PARTICULARLY COMPLEX MIND.. FOLLOWING NO CLEAR LOGICAL PATH, HE CAME TO THE TEST OF EXPERIMENT..
HE COLLECTED HIS MIND... RESOLUTE.. SAYS TO THE CANDLE..
..BE RAISED UP!!..

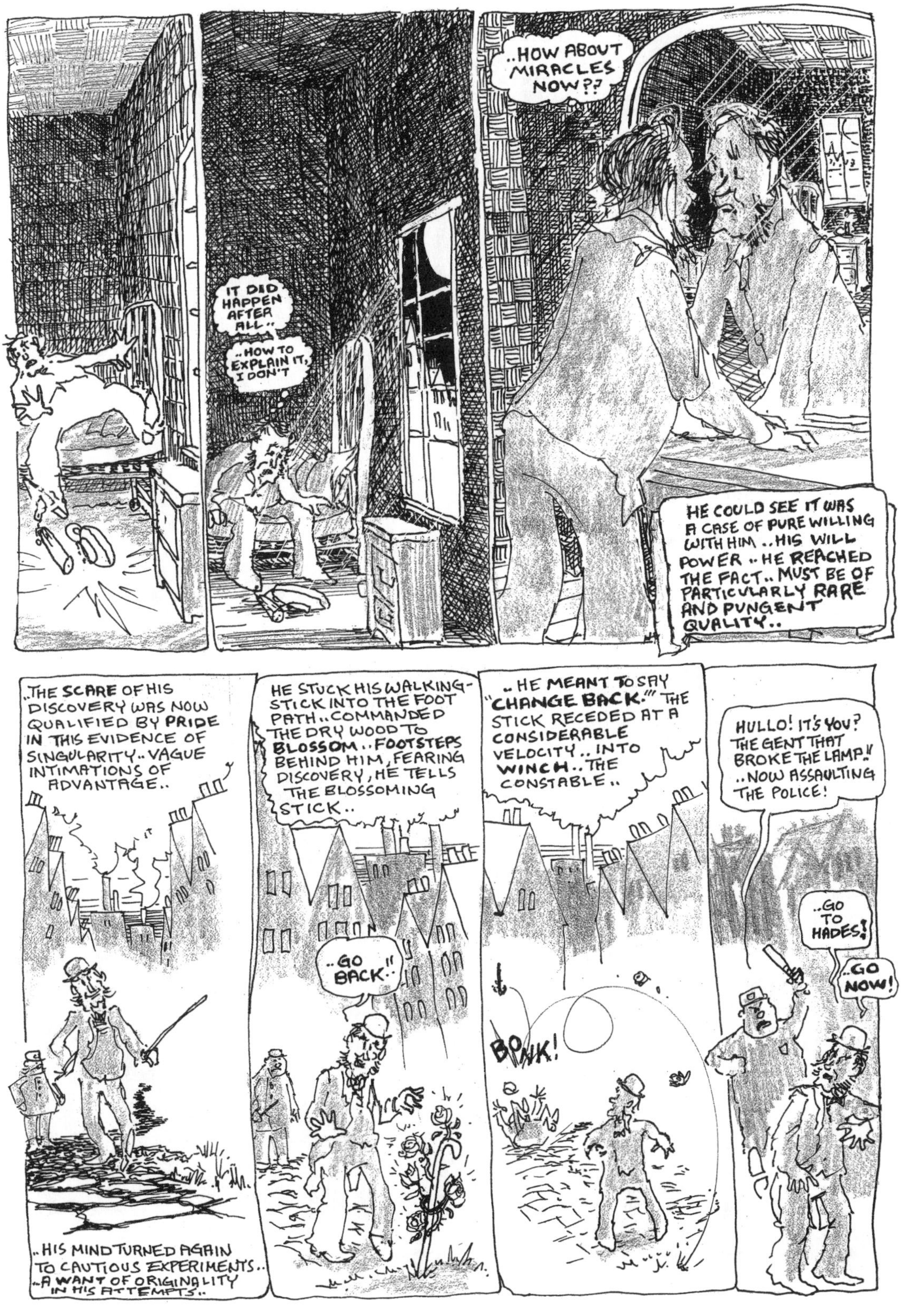
IT DID HAPPEN AFTER ALL..
..HOW TO EXPLAIN IT, I DON'T
..HOW ABOUT MIRACLES NOW?!?
HE COULD SEE IT WAS A CASE OF PURE WILLING WITH HIM..HIS WILL POWER .. HE REACHED THE FACT.. MUST BE OF PARTICULARLY RARE AND PUNGENT QUALITY..
..THE SCARE OF HIS DISCOVERY WAS NOW QUALIFIED BY PRIDE IN THIS EVIDENCE OF SINGULARITY.. VAGUE INTIMATIONS OF ADVANTAGE..
..HIS MIND TURNED AGAIN TO CAUTIOUS EXPERIMENTS.. ..A WANT OF ORIGINALITY IN HIS ATTEMPTS..
HE STUCK HIS WALKING-STICK INTO THE FOOT PATH.. COMMANDED THE DRY WOOD TO BLOSSOM.. FOOTSTEPS BEHIND HIM, FEARING DISCOVERY, HE TELLS THE BLOSSOMING STICK..
..GO BACK."
.. HE MEANT TO SAY "CHANGE BACK."" THE STICK RECEDED AT A CONSIDERABLE VELOCITY.. INTO WINCH.. THE CONSTABLE..
BONK!
HULLO! IT'S YOU? THE GENT THAT BROKE THE LAMP!! ..NOW ASSAULTING THE POLICE!
..GO TO HADES!
..GO NOW!

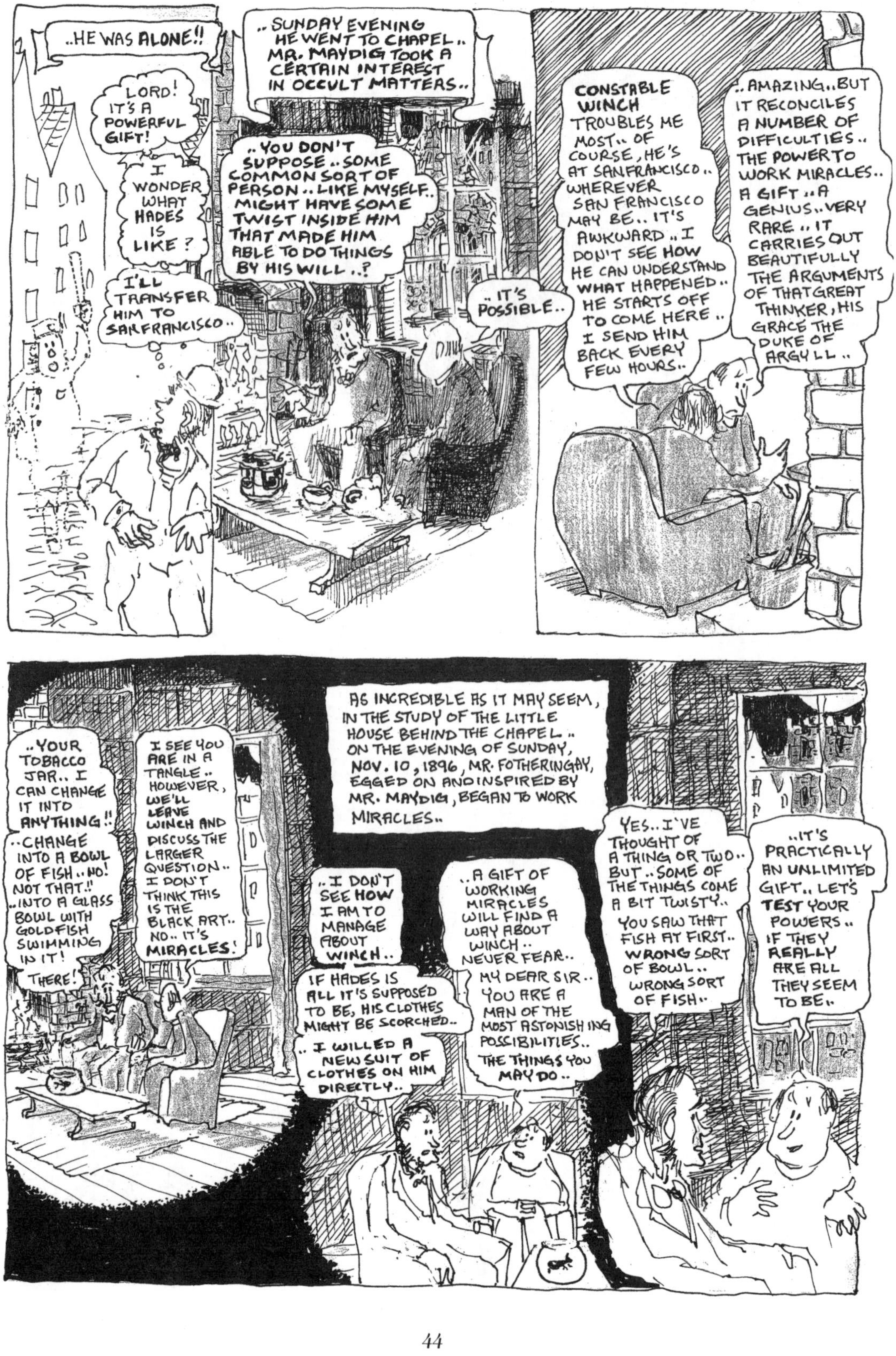
..HE WAS ALONE!!
LORD! IT'S A POWERFUL GIFT!
I WONDER WHAT HADES IS LIKE?
I'LL TRANSFER HIM TO SAN FRANCISCO..
..SUNDAY EVENING HE WENT TO CHAPEL.. MR. MAYDIG TOOK A CERTAIN INTEREST IN OCCULT MATTERS..
..YOU DON'T SUPPOSE..SOME COMMON SORT OF PERSON..LIKE MYSELF..MIGHT HAVE SOME TWIST INSIDE HIM THAT MADE HIM ABLE TO DO THINGS BY HIS WILL..?
..IT'S POSSIBLE..
CONSTABLE WINCH TROUBLES ME MOST.. OF COURSE, HE'S AT SAN FRANCISCO.. WHEREVER SAN FRANCISCO MAY BE.. IT'S AWKWARD.. I DON'T SEE HOW HE CAN UNDERSTAND WHAT HAPPENED.. HE STARTS OFF TO COME HERE.. I SEND HIM BACK EVERY FEW HOURS..
..AMAZING..BUT IT RECONCILES A NUMBER OF DIFFICULTIES.. THE POWER TO WORK MIRACLES.. A GIFT..A GENIUS..VERY RARE.. IT CARRIES OUT BEAUTIFULLY THE ARGUMENTS OF THAT GREAT THINKER, HIS GRACE THE DUKE OF ARGYLL..
AS INCREDIBLE AS IT MAY SEEM, IN THE STUDY OF THE LITTLE HOUSE BEHIND THE CHAPEL.. ON THE EVENING OF SUNDAY, NOV. 10, 1896, MR. FOTHERINGAY, EGGED ON AND INSPIRED BY MR. MAYDIG, BEGAN TO WORK MIRACLES..
..YOUR TOBACCO JAR.. I CAN CHANGE IT INTO ANYTHING!!
..CHANGE INTO A BOWL OF FISH..NO! NOT THAT!! ..INTO A GLASS BOWL WITH GOLDFISH SWIMMING IN IT!
THERE!
I SEE YOU ARE IN A TANGLE.. HOWEVER, WE'LL LEAVE WINCH AND DISCUSS THE LARGER QUESTION.. I DON'T THINK THIS IS THE BLACK ART.. NO.. IT'S MIRACLES!
..I DON'T SEE HOW I AM TO MANAGE ABOUT WINCH..
IF HADES IS ALL IT'S SUPPOSED TO BE, HIS CLOTHES MIGHT BE SCORCHED..
..I WILLED A NEW SUIT OF CLOTHES ON HIM DIRECTLY..
..A GIFT OF WORKING MIRACLES WILL FIND A WAY ABOUT WINCH.. NEVER FEAR..
MY DEAR SIR.. YOU ARE A MAN OF THE MOST ASTONISHING POSSIBILITIES.. THE THINGS YOU MAY DO..
YES..I'VE THOUGHT OF A THING OR TWO.. BUT..SOME OF THE THINGS COME A BIT TWISTY.. YOU SAW THAT FISH AT FIRST.. WRONG SORT OF BOWL.. WRONG SORT OF FISH..
..IT'S PRACTICALLY AN UNLIMITED GIFT.. LET'S TEST YOUR POWERS.. IF THEY REALLY ARE ALL THEY SEEM TO BE.

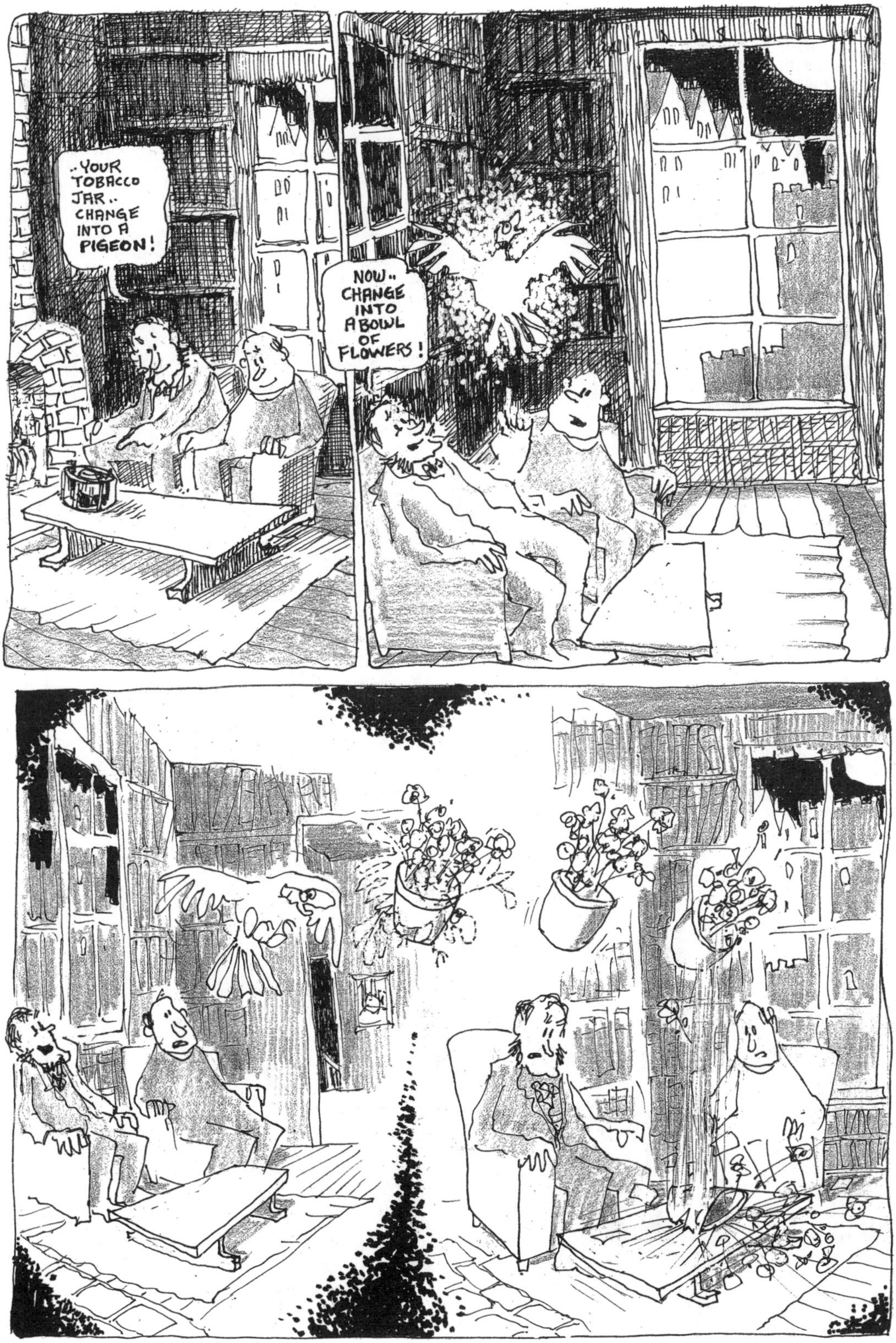
..YOUR TOBACCO JAR.. CHANGE INTO A PIGEON!
NOW.. CHANGE INTO A BOWL OF FLOWERS!

NOV. 10, 1896.. THE READER'S ATTENTION IS SPECIALLY CALLED TO THAT DATE.. HE WILL OBJECT.. CERTAIN POINTS IN THIS STORY ARE IMPROBABLE.. IF ANYTHING ALREADY DESCRIBED HAD OCCURRED, THEY'D HAVE BEEN IN THE PAPERS A YEAR AGO..

.. THE DETAILS FOLLOWING WILL BE HARD TO ACCEPT.. .. BECAUSE THEY INVOLVE THE CONCLUSION THAT HE OR SHE, THE READER IN QUESTION, MUST HAVE DIED IN A VIOLENT MANNER MORE THAN A YEAR AGO..

NOW A MIRACLE IS NOTHING IF NOT IMPROBABLE .. AS A MATTER OF FACT, THE READER WAS KILLED IN A VIOLENT AND UNPRECEDENTED MANNER A YEAR AGO.. IN THE COURSE OF THIS STORY, THAT WILL BECOME CLEAR AND CREDIBLE..

.. BUT THIS IS NOT THE PLACE FOR THE END OF THE STORY.. .. BEING BUT A LITTLE BEYOND THE HITHER SIDE OF THE MIDDLE.. .. AT FIRST, THE MIRACLES WORKED BY MR. FOTHERINGAY WERE TIMID LITTLE THINGS.. .. FEEBLE AS THEY WERE, THEY WERE RECEIVED WITH AWE BY HIS COLLABORATOR, MR. MAYDIG..

.. AFTER THEY HAD WORKED A DOZEN OF THESE DOMESTIC TRIVIALITIES, THEIR SENSE OF POWER GREW..

THEIR IMAGINATION BEGAN TO SHOW SIGNS OF STIMULATION.. THEIR AMBITION ENLARGED.. THEIR FIRST LARGER ENTERPRISE WAS DUE TO HUNGER.. AND THE NEGLIGENCE OF MRS. MINCHIN, MR. MAYDIG'S HOUSEKEEPER.. THE MEAL WAS ILL-LAID AND UNINVITING AS REFRESHMENT FOR TWO INDUSTRIOUS MIRACLE WORKERS.. MR. MAYDIG WAS DESCANTING IN SORROW UPON HIS HOUSEKEEPER'S SHORTCOMINGS BEFORE IT OCCURRED TO MR. FOTHERINGAY AN OPPORTUNITY LAY BEFORE HIM..

.. A BURGUNDY?

DON'T YOU THINK, MR. MAYDIG.. IF IT ISN'T A LIBERTY ..?

MR. FOTHERINGAY WAVED HIS HAND.. "WHAT SHALL WE HAVE?" HE SAID, IN A LARGE, INCLUSIVE SPIRIT.. AT MR. MAYDIG'S ORDER, HE REVISED THE SUPPER VERY THROUGHLY..

.. AS FOR ME, I'M FOND OF A TANKARD OF STOUT AND A NICE WELSH RABBIT..

"I SAY.." SAID MR. FOTHERINGAY.."THAT'S **THREE O'CLOCK**! I MUST BE GETTING BACK.. I'VE GOT TO BE AT BUSINESS BY EIGHT.."

"WE'RE ONLY JUST BEGINNING.."SAID MR. MAYDIG.." THINK OF ALL THE **GOOD** WE'RE DOING.. WHEN PEOPLE WAKE.."

..MY DEAR CHAP.. THERE'S NO HURRY.. **LOOK!!**

JOSHUA!

JOSHUA?

"JOSHUA?" SAID MR. FOTHERINGAY.. "JOSHUA.." SAID MR. MAYDIG.. "WHY NOT? **STOP** IT!"

MR. FOTHERINGAY LOOKED AT THE MOON.. "THAT'S A BIT **TALL**.." HE SAID..

"WHY NOT?" SAID MR. MAYDIG.. "OF COURSE, IT DOESN'T STOP.. YOU STOP THE **ROTATION** OF THE EARTH, YOU KNOW.. TIME STOPS.. IT ISN'T AS IF WE WERE DOING **HARM**.."

HMM.. WELL..?

..I'LL TRY..

HERE! ..JEST STOP ROTATING, WILL YOU!!

INCONTINENTLY HE WAS FLYING HEAD OVER HEELS AT THE RATE OF DOZENS OF MILES A MINUTE.. HE THOUGHT IN A SECOND, AND WILLED.. "LET ME COME DOWN SAFE AND SOUND.."

"WHATEVER ELSE HAPPENS, LET ME COME DOWN SAFE AND SOUND..."

FAR AND WIDE.. NOTHING WAS VISIBLE.. TUMBLED
MASSES OF EARTH.. **INCHOATE RUINS**.. NO TREES..
NO HOUSES.. NO FAMILIAR **SHAPES**.. ONLY A
WILDERNESS OF DISORDER.. VANISHING INTO THE
DARKNESS..

YOU SEE, WHEN MR. FOTHERINGAY HAD ARRESTED
THE ROTATION OF THE SOLID GLOBE, HE HAD MADE
NO STIPULATION CONCERNING THE **TRIFLING**
MOVABLES UPON ITS SURFACE.. THE EARTH SPINS
SO FAST THE SURFACE AT ITS EQUATOR IS TRAVELLING
AT RATHER MORE THAN A THOUSAND MILES AN HOUR..

SO.. THE VILLAGE, MR. MAYDIG, MR. FOTHERINGAY,
EVERYBODY AND EVERYTHING HAD BEEN JERKED
VIOLENTLY FORWARD.. AT ABOUT **NINE MILES**
PER SECOND!! MORE VIOLENTLY THAN IF THEY
HAD BEEN FIRED OUT OF A CANNON.. EVERY
LIVING CREATURE.. JERKED, AND SMASHED
AND UTTERLY DESTROYED..

.. THAT WAS
   ALL ..

".. AND NOW WHAT DO I DO?.. I KNOW.. AND FOR
GOODNESS SAKE, LET'S GET IT **RIGHT THIS TIME**..
.. AH.. LET NOTHING WHAT I'M GOING TO ORDER HAPPEN
UNTIL I SAY '**OFF!**' LORD, I WISH I THOUGHT OF
THAT BEFORE.. NOW THEN.. HERE GOES.. LET ME **LOSE**
MY MIRACULOUS POWER.. LET ME BE JUST AS IT WAS
BEFORE THAT BLESSED LAMP TURNED UP.. HAVE YOU
GOT IT? **NO MORE MIRACLES**!.. ME BACK JUST
BEFORE I DRANK MY HALF PINT.. "

.. HE CLOSED HIS EYES.. AND SAID.. "OFF!"

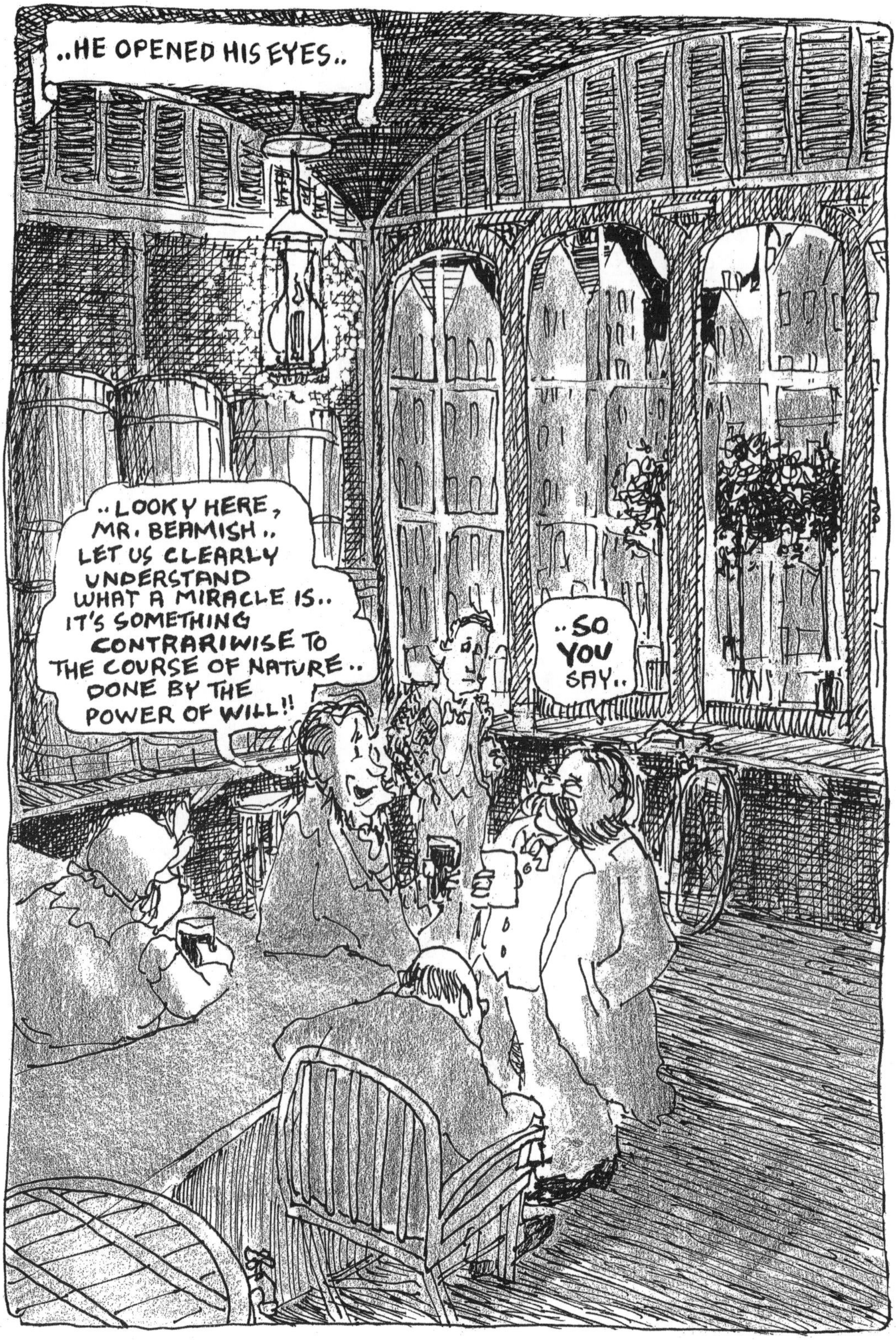
..HE OPENED HIS EYES..
..LOOKY HERE, MR. BEAMISH.. LET US CLEARLY UNDERSTAND WHAT A MIRACLE IS.. IT'S SOMETHING CONTRARIWISE TO THE COURSE OF NATURE.. DONE BY THE POWER OF WILL!!
..SO YOU SAY..

A Moonlight Fable

illustrated by

SHARY FLENNIKEN

©2002 SHARY FLENNIKEN

Story by H.G. Wells

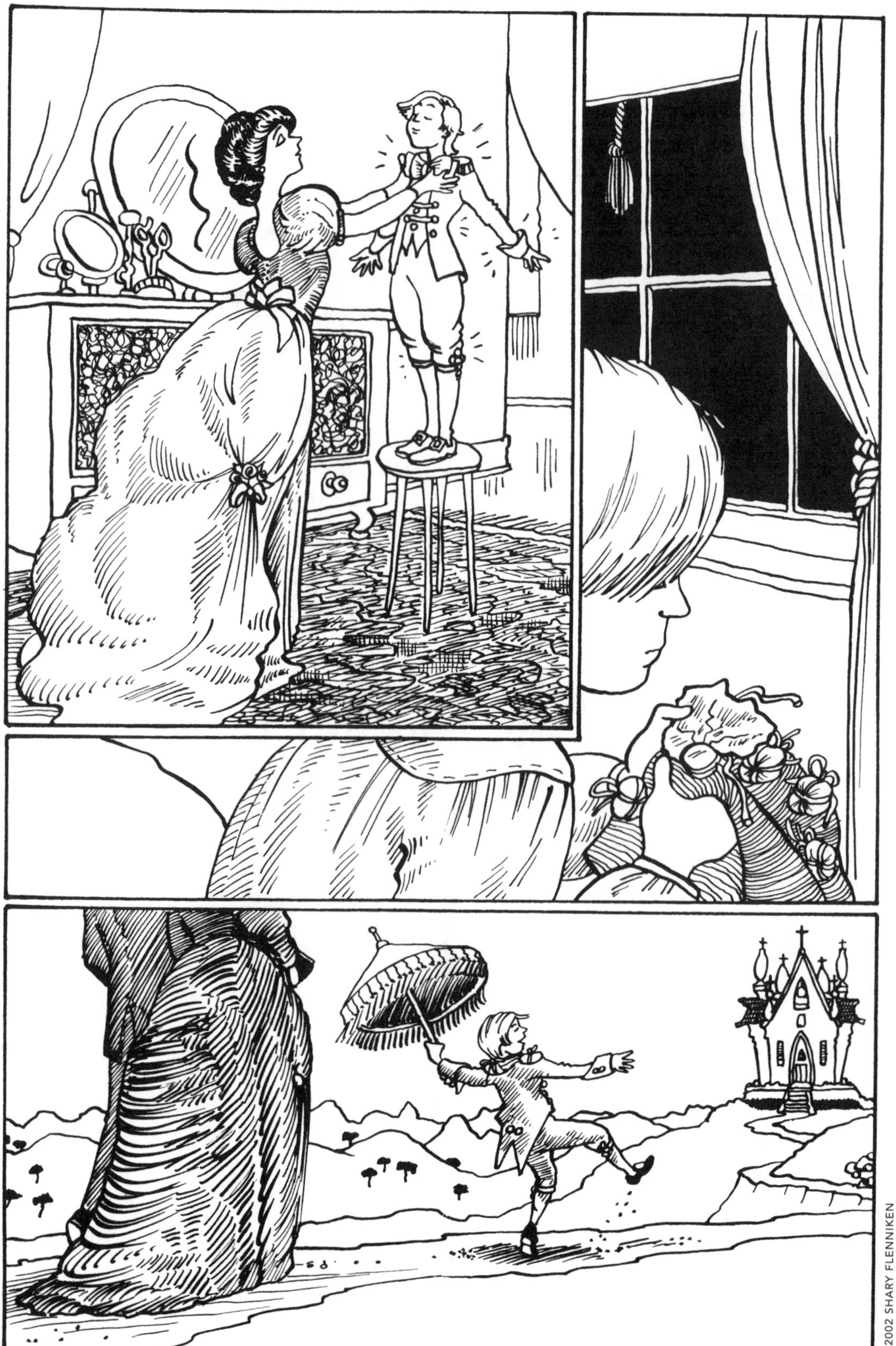

There was once a little man whose mother made him a beautiful suit of clothes. It was green and gold and woven so that I cannot describe how delicate and fine it was, and there was a tie of orange fluffiness that tied up under his chin. And the buttons in their newness shone like stars. He was proud and pleased by his suit beyond measure, and stood before the long looking glass when first he put it on, so astonished and delighted with it that he could hardly turn himself away.

He wanted to wear it everywhere and show it to all sorts of people. He thought over all the places he had ever visited and all the scenes he had ever heard described, and tried to imagine what the feel of it would be if he were to go now to those scenes and places wearing his shining suit, and he wanted to go out forthwith into the long grass and the hot sunshine of the meadow wearing it. Just to wear it! But his mother told him, "No." She told him he must take great care of his suit, for never would he have another nearly so fine; he must save it and save it and only wear it on rare and great occasions. It was his wedding suit, she said. And she took his buttons and twisted them up with tissue paper for fear their bright newness should be tarnished, and she tacked little guards over the cuffs and elbows and wherever the suit was most likely to come to harm. He hated and resisted these things, but what could he do? And at last her warnings and persuasions had effect and he consented to take off his beautiful suit and fold it into its proper creases and put it away. It was almost as though he gave it up again. But he was always thinking of wearing it and of the supreme occasion when some day it might be worn without the guards, without the tissue paper on the buttons, utterly and delightfully, never caring, beautiful beyond measure.

One night when he was dreaming of it, after his habit, he dreamed he took the tissue paper from one of the buttons and found its brightness a little faded, and that distressed him mightily in his dream. He polished the poor faded button and polished it, and if anything it grew duller. He woke up and lay awake thinking of the brightness a little dulled and wondering how he would feel if perhaps when the great occasion (whatever it might be) should arrive, one button should chance to be ever so little short of its first glittering freshness, and for days and days that thought remained with him, distressingly. And when next his mother let him wear his suit, he was tempted and nearly gave way to the temptation just to fumble off one little bit of tissue paper and see if indeed the buttons were keeping as bright as ever.

He went trimly along on his way to church full of this wild desire. For you must know his mother did, with repeated and careful warnings, let him wear his suit at times, on Sundays, for example, to and fro from church, when there was no threatening of rain, no dust nor anything to injure it, with its buttons covered and its protections tacked upon it and a sunshade in his hand to shadow it if there seemed too strong a sunlight for its colours. And always, after such occasions, he brushed it over and folded it exquisitely as she had taught him, and put it away again.

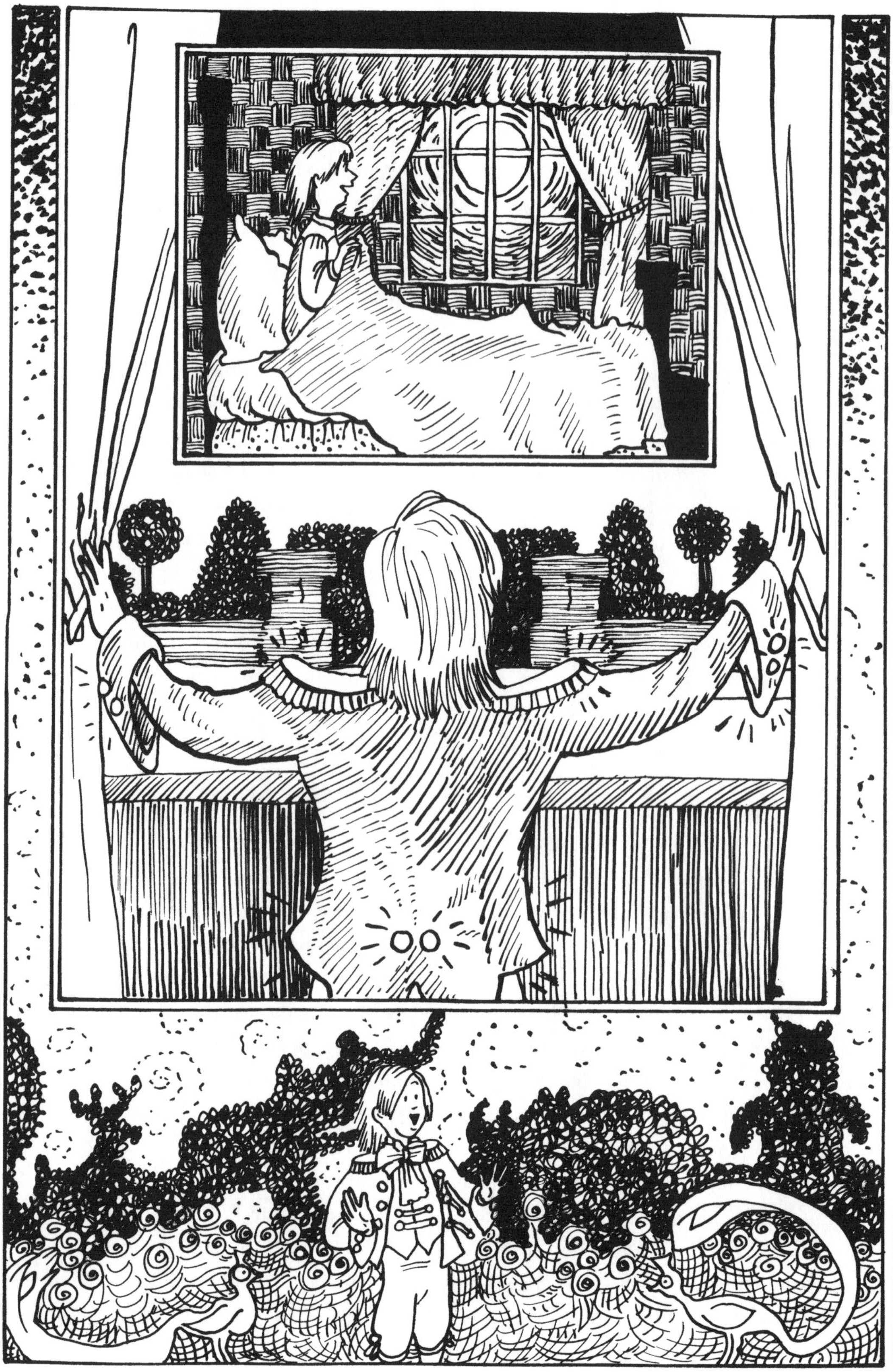
©2002 SHARY FLENNIKEN

Now all these restrictions his mother set to the wearing of his suit he obeyed, always he obeyed them, until one strange night he woke up and saw the moonlight shining outside his window. It seemed to him the moonlight was not common moonlight, nor the night a common night, and for a while he lay quite drowsily with this odd persuasion in his mind. Thought joined onto thought like things that whisper warmly in the shadows. Then he sat up in his little bed suddenly, very alert, with his heart beating very fast and a quiver in his body from top to toe. He had made up his mind. He knew now that he was going to wear his suit as it should be worn. He had no doubt in the matter. He was afraid, terribly afraid, but glad, glad.

He got out of his bed and stood a moment by the window looking at the moon-shine-flooded garden and trembling at the thing he meant to do. The air was full of a minute clamor of crickets and murmurings, of the infinitesimal shouting of little living things. He went very gently across the creaking boards, for fear that he might wake the sleeping house, to the big dark clothes-press wherein his beautiful suit lay folded, and he took it out garment by garment and softly and very eagerly tore off its tissue-paper covering and its tacked protections, until there it was, perfect and delightful as he had seen it when first his mother had given it to him— a long time it seemed ago. Not a button had tarnished, not a thread had faded on this dear suit of his; he was glad enough for weeping as in a noiseless hurry he put it on. And then back he went, soft and quick, to the window and looked out upon the garden and stood there for a minute, shining in the moonlight, with his buttons twinkling like stars, before he got out on the sill and, making as little of a rustling as he could, clambered down to the garden path below. He stood before his mother's house, and it was white and nearly as plain as by day, with every window-blind but his own shut like an eye that sleeps. The trees cast still shadows like intricate black lace upon the wall.

The garden in the moonlight was very different from the garden by day; moonshine was tangled in the hedges and stretched in phantom cobwebs from spray to spray. Every flower was gleaming white or crimson black, and the air was aquiver with the thridding of small crickets and nightingales singing unseen in the depths of the trees.

There was no darkness in the world, but only warm, mysterious shadows; and all the leaves and spikes were edged and lined with iridescent jewels of dew. The night was warmer than any night had ever been, the heavens by some miracle at once vaster and nearer, and in spite of the great ivory-tinted moon that ruled the world, the sky was full of stars.

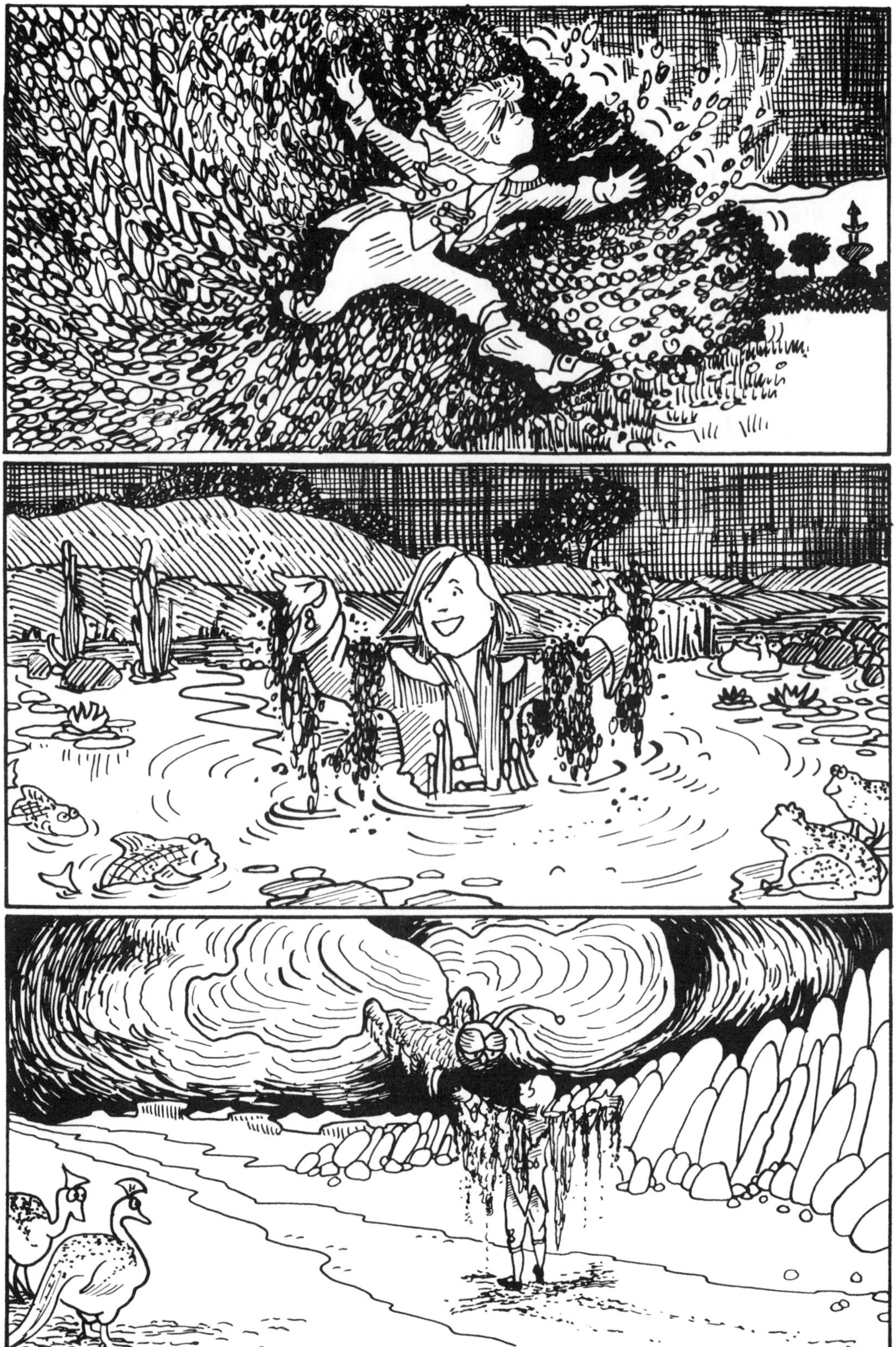
©02 SHARY FLENNIKEN

The little man did not shout nor sing for all his infinite gladness. He stood for a time like one awe-stricken, and then, with a queer small cry and holding out his arms, he ran out as if he would embrace at once the whole warm round immensity of the world. He did not follow the neat set paths that cut the garden squarely, but thrust across the beds and through the wet, tall, scented herbs, through the night stock and the nicotine and the clusters of phantom white mallow flowers and through the thickets of southern-wood and lavender, and knee-deep across a wide space of mignonette. He came to the great hedge and he thrust his way through it, and though the thorns of the brambles scored him deeply and tore threads from his wonderful suit, and though burs and goosegrass and havers caught and clung to him, he did not care. He did not care, for he knew it was all part of the wearing for which he had longed. "I am glad I put on my suit," he said; "I am glad I wore my suit."

Beyond the hedge he came to the duck-pond, or at least to what was the duck-pond by day. But by night it was a great bowl of silver moonshine all noisy with singing frogs, of wonderful silver moonshine twisted and clotted with strange patternings, and the little man ran down into its waters between the thin black rushes, knee-deep and waist-deep and to his shoulders, smiting the water to black and shining wavelets with either hand, swaying and shivering wavelets, amid which the stars were netted in the tangled reflections of the brooding trees upon the bank. He waded until he swam, and so he crossed the pond and came out upon the other side, trailing, as it seemed to him, not duckweed, but very silver in long, clinging, dripping masses. And up he went through the transfigured tangles of the willow-herb and the uncut seeding grass of the farther bank. And so he came glad and breathless into the highroad. "I am glad," he said, "beyond measure, that I had clothes that fitted this occasion."

The highroad ran straight as an arrow flies, straight into the deep blue pit of sky beneath the moon, a white and shining road between the singing nightingales, and along it he went, running now and leaping, and now walking and rejoicing, in the clothes his mother had made for him with tireless, loving hands. The road was deep in dust, but that for him was only soft whiteness, and as he went a great dim moth came fluttering round his wet and shimmering and hastening figure. At first he did not heed the moth, and then he waved his hands at it and made a sort of dance with it as it circled round his head. "Soft moth!" he cried, "dear moth! And wonderful night, wonderful night of the world! Do you think my clothes are beautiful, dear moth? As beautiful as your scales and all this silver vesture of the earth and sky?"

And the moth circled closer and closer until at last its velvet wings just brushed his lips...

And next morning they found him dead with his neck broken in the bottom of the stone pit, with his beautiful clothes a little bloody and foul and stained with the duckweed from the pond. But his face was a face of such happiness that, had you seen it, you would have understood indeed how that he had died happy, never knowing the cool and streaming silver for the duckweed in the pond. ✒

The MAN with a NOSE

illustrated by

SKIP WILLIAMSON

Story by H.G. Wells

My nose has been the curse of my life.

The other man started.

They had not spoken before. They were sitting, one at either end, on that seat on the stony summit of Primrose Hill which looks towards Regent's Park. It was night. The paths on the slope below were dotted out by yellow lamps; the Albert-road was a line of faintly luminous pale green—the tint of gaslight seen among trees; beyond, the park lay black and mysterious, and still further, a yellow mist beneath and a coppery hue in the sky above marked the blaze of the Marylebone thoroughfares. The nearer houses in the Albert-terrace loomed large and black, their blackness pierced irregularly by luminous windows. Above, starlight.

Both men had been silent, lost apparently in their own thoughts, mere dim black figures to each other, until one had seen fit to become a voice also, with this confidence.

Yes...

He said, after an interval.

My nose has always stood in my way, always.

The second man had scarcely seemed to notice the first remark, but now he peered through the night at his interlocutor. It was a little man he saw, with face turned towards him.

I see nothing wrong with your nose.

If it were luminous you might.

However, I will illuminate it.

He fumbled with something in his pocket, then held this object in his hand. There was a scratch, a streak of greenish phosphorescent light, and then all the world beyond became black, as a fusee vesta flared.

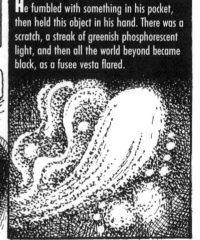

There was silence for the space of a minute. An impressive pause.

Well?

I have seen worse.

I doubt it...

...and even so, it is poor comfort. Did you notice the shape? the size? the colour? Like Snowdon, it has a steep side and a gentle slope. The size is preposterous; my face is like a hen-house built behind a portico.

And the tints!

59

It is not all red...

...anyhow.

"No, there is purple, and blue, lapis lazuli, blue as a vein over the Madonna's breast, and in one place a greyish mole. Bah! The thing is not a nose at all, but a bit of primordial chaos clapped onto my face. But, being where the nose should be, it gets the credit of its position from unthinking people. There is a gap in the order of the universe in front of my face, a lump of unwrought material left over. In that my true nose is hidden, as a statue is hidden in a lump of marble, until the appointed time for the revelation shall come. At the resurrection — But one must not anticipate. Well, well. I do not often talk about my nose, my friend, but you sat with a sympathetic pose, it seemed to me, and to-night my heart is full of it. This cursed nose! But do I weary you, thrusting my nose into your meditations?"

"If," said the second man, his voice a little unsteady, as though he was moved...

If it eases your mind to talk of your nose, pray talk.

"This nose, I say then, makes me think of the false noses of Carnival times. Your dullest man has but to stick one on, and lo! mirth, wit, and jollity. They are enough to make anything funny. I doubt if even an Anglican bishop could wear one with impunity. Put an angel in one. How would you like one popped onto you now? Think of going lovemaking, or addressing a public meeting, or dying gloriously, in a nose like mine! Angelina laughs in your face, the public laughs, the executioner at your martyrdom can hardly light the faggots for laughing. By heaven! It is no joke. Often and often I have rebelled, and said, 'I will not have this nose'"

But what can one do?

"It is destiny. The bitter tragedy of it is that it is so comic. Only, God knows, how glad I shall be when the Carnival is over, and I may take the thing off and put it aside. The worst has been this business of love. My mind is not unrefined, my body is healthy. I know what tenderness is. But what woman could overlook a nose like mine? How could she shut out her visions of it, and look her love into my eyes, glaring at her over its immensity? I should have to make love through an Inquisitor's hood, with its holes cut for the eyes — and even then the shape would show. I have read, I have been told, I can imagine what a lover's face is like — a sweet woman's face radiant with love."

"But this Millbank penitentiary of flesh chills their dear hearts."

⊙?✳!# Ssh!

He broke off suddenly, with loud ferocious curses. A young man who had been sitting very close to a young woman on an adjacent seat, started up and said...

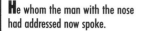 He whom the man with the nose had addressed now spoke.

I have certainly never thought before of a red nose as a sorrowful thing, but as you put it...

"I thought you would understand. I have had this nose all my life. The outline was done, even though the colour was wanting, in my school days. They called me...

 Nosey! Ovid! Cicero! Rhino! And the Excrescence!

"It has ripened with the slow years, as fate deepens in the progress of a tragedy.

"Love, the business of life, is a sealed book to me.

 "To be alone! I would thank heaven.

"But no!

GRRRR!

"A blind woman could feel the shape of it."

"Besides love," interrupted the young man thoughtfully, "there are other things worth living for. Duty. An unattractive nose would not interfere with that. Some people think it is rather more important than love."

"That only carries out the evidence of your voice, and tells me you are young. My dear young fellow, duty is a very fine thing indeed, but believe me, it is too colourless as a motive. There is no delight in duty. You will know that at my age. And besides, I have an infinite capacity for love and sympathy, an infinite bitterness in this solitude of my soul. I infer that you would moralise on my discontent, but I know I have seen a little of men and things from behind this ambuscade – only a truly artistic man would fall into the sympathetic attitude that attracted me. My life has had even too much of observation in it, and to the systematic anthropologist, nothing tells a man's character more than his pose after dark, when nobody seems watching. As you sit, the black outline of you is clear against the sky. Ah! now you are sitting stiffer. But you are no Calvinist. My friend, the best of life is its delights, and the best of delights is loving and being loved. And for that – this nose! Well, there are plenty of second-best things. After dark I can forget the monster a little. Spring is delightful, air on the Downs is delightful; it is fine to see the stars circling in the sky, while lying among the heather. Even this London sky is soothing at night, though the edge is all inflamed."

 I admit your loss, of course.

The shadow of my nose is darkest by day. But tonight I am bitter, because of tomorrow.

 Why, tomorrow?

"I have to meet some new people tomorrow," said the man with the nose. "There is an odd look, a mingling of amusement and pity, I am only too familiar with.

"My cousin, who is a gifted hostess, promises people my nose as a treat."

Yes, that must be bad for you.

And then the silence healed again, and presently the man with the nose got up and passed into the dimness upon the slope of the hill. The young man watched him vanish, wondering vainly how it would be possible to console a soul under such a burden.

 END

©2002 SKIP WILLIAMSON

In the Abyss

adapted and illustrated by

JOHN PIERARD

Story by H.G. Wells

JANUARY 5, 1896. THE FREIGHTER SOUTHERN STAR WAS ANCHORED AT SEA IN SOUTHERN WATERS.

IT'S FIVE MILES DOWN TO THE BOTTOM, ELSTEAD. THINK OF THE PRESSURE! IT'LL CRACK YOUR SPHERE LIKE AN EGGSHELL AND SPREAD YOU ACROSS THE INSIDE LIKE BUTTER ON BREAD.

I'VE DONE THE CALCULATIONS, CAPTAIN WHEYBRIDGE, AND I'LL TAKE MY CHANCES.

AND WHAT MIGHT THAT BE THAT YOU'VE BEEN TINKERING ON WITH SUCH CARE?

THIS IS THE CLOCKWORK MECHANISM THAT WILL BRING THE SPHERE BACK TO THE SURFACE.

63

"YOU SEE, I'M USING A HEAVY WEIGHT TO DRAG THE SPHERE TO THE BOTTOM. WITHOUT IT, MY CRAFT WOULD JUST FLOAT ON THE SURFACE.

"THE WEIGHT IS ATTACHED TO THE SPHERE BY A LONG CORD. IT WILL HIT BOTTOM FIRST AND ABSORB THE SHOCK OF IMPACT."

THAT WILL TRIGGER THE MOTOR, WHICH WILL WIND UP THE CORD, AND BRING THE SPHERE DOWN THE REST OF THE WAY.

WHEN THE SPHERE HAS TOUCHED BOTTOM, THE CLOCKWORK WILL START TO TICK OFF A HALF HOUR. AT THE END OF THAT TIME, A SPRING-LOADED KNIFE WILL CUT THE CORD ATTACHED TO THE WEIGHT, AND UP I SHALL RUSH LIKE A BUBBLE IN A POP BOTTLE.

ON THE MORNING OF JANUARY 6, ELSTEAD PREPARED TO MAKE HIS HISTORIC JOURNEY TO THE OCEAN FLOOR.

THE SPHERE, WHICH LOOKED SO LARGE ON DECK, APPEARED TINY AS IT WAS GENTLY LOWERED. ELSTEAD WAS ALREADY INSIDE.

AT ELSTEAD'S SIGNAL THE CREW RELEASED THE LINE. THEY GAVE SILENT PRAYER AS THE SPHERE VANISHED BENEATH THE WAVES.

A HALF HOUR CAME AND WENT. THE SUN ROSE HIGH IN THE SKY, AND THEN SANK TOWARD EVENING. AND STILL NO SIGN OF ELSTEAD.

ELSTEAD-- WHERE ARE YOU?

TWELVE HOURS PASSED. THEN, A SPECK OF LIGHT WAS SEEN LEAPING FROM THE SEA, A SHORT DISTANCE FROM THE SHIP.

THE SPHERE WAS TAKEN ABOARD. WHEN IT WAS OPENED, ELSTEAD WAS THERE... UNCONSCIOUS.

IT WAS NEARLY A WEEK BEFORE HE WAS STRONG ENOUGH TO TELL HIS STORY.

IT ALL BEGAN RATHER DREADFULLY. ALL THAT ROLLING AROUND IN THE WATER...

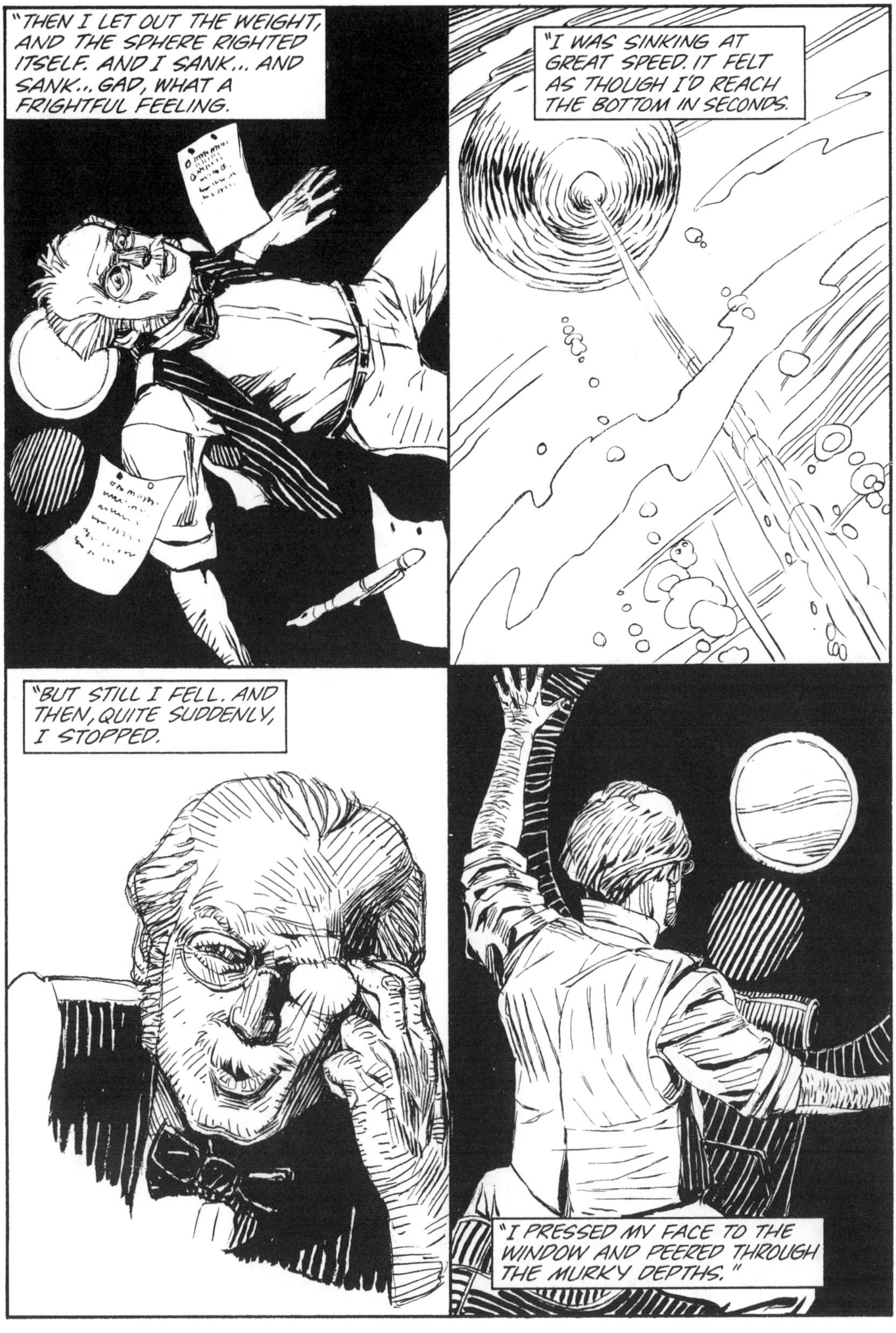
"THEN I LET OUT THE WEIGHT, AND THE SPHERE RIGHTED ITSELF. AND I SANK... AND SANK... GAD, WHAT A FRIGHTFUL FEELING.
"I WAS SINKING AT GREAT SPEED. IT FELT AS THOUGH I'D REACH THE BOTTOM IN SECONDS.
"BUT STILL I FELL. AND THEN, QUITE SUDDENLY, I STOPPED.
"I PRESSED MY FACE TO THE WINDOW AND PEERED THROUGH THE MURKY DEPTHS."

"A REMARKABLE LANDSCAPE LAY BEFORE ME, LIT BY A GHOSTLY GLEAM. I WAS NOT PREPARED FOR WHAT HAPPENED NEXT...

"MOVING TOWARDS ME WAS A FIGURE. SURELY IT WAS NO FISH.

"I SWITCHED ON THE OUTSIDE LIGHT. MY BLOOD FROZE. THE CREATURE WAS... ALMOST... HUMAN!"

"I HEARD IT CALLING, BUT COULD MAKE NO SENSE OF WHAT IT SAID.

"THEN, ONE BY ONE, MORE OF THE CREATURES APPEARED. SOON, I WAS SURROUNDED."

"THEY CLIMBED ATOP MY SPHERE, AND PEERED THROUGH THE WINDOW WITH COLD, REPTILIAN EYES.

"IN ANOTHER MOMENT, HANDS BEGAN POUNDING ON THE METAL HULL. I FEARED FOR MY LIFE.

"ALL OF A SUDDEN, I FELT THE SPHERE BEGIN TO RISE. I HAD NO IDEA OF WHAT WAS HAPPENING."

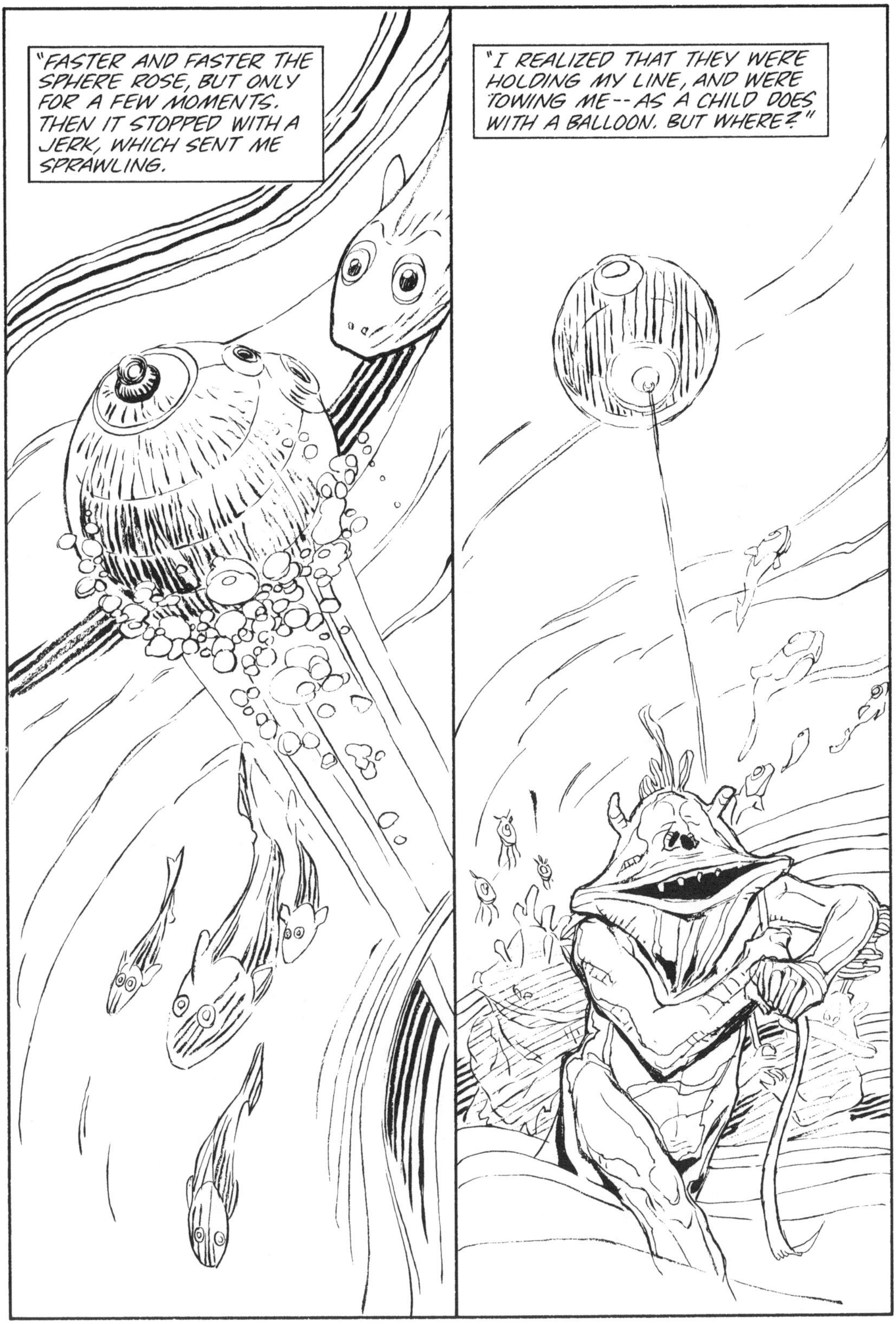
"FASTER AND FASTER THE SPHERE ROSE, BUT ONLY FOR A FEW MOMENTS. THEN IT STOPPED WITH A JERK, WHICH SENT ME SPRAWLING.
"I REALIZED THAT THEY WERE HOLDING MY LINE, AND WERE TOWING ME--AS A CHILD DOES WITH A BALLOON. BUT WHERE?"

"I SAW THE REMAINS OF MANY WRECKED SHIPS. TWISTED TIMBERS AND IRON BEAMS LITTERED THE GHOSTLY LANDSCAPE.

"SOON I WAS FLOATING OVER AN UNDERSEA CITY. THE BUILDINGS WERE HUGE AND ROOFLESS..."

"... THE CITY WAS CONSTRUCTED OF PARTS FROM SHIPS, AND ROW AFTER ROW OF GLOWING HUMAN BONES AND SKULLS.

"THE WHOLE PLACE HAD AN EERIE GLOW, LIKE DROWNED MOONLIGHT. I COULD NOW SEE THOUSANDS OF THE CREATURES.

"IT WAS LIKE SOME FANTASTIC DREAM. I WAS MORE FASCINATED THAN FRIGHTENED."

"I PEERED THROUGH THE WINDOW, AND WATCHED AS I WAS DRAGGED TOWARD A LARGE BUILDING IN WHAT SEEMED TO BE THE CENTER OF THEIR CITY.

"I BELIEVE IT WAS A CATHEDRAL OF SOME KIND. BUT ITS SURFACE WAS LINED WITH ZIG-ZAGS AND SPIRALS OF HUMAN SKULLS.

"SILENTLY, WE CAME TO A STOP."

"MY SPHERE WAS PLACED ON A BROAD PEDESTAL. I MUST HAVE APPEARED TO THEM AS A GIFT FROM A GOD, SENT DOWN THROUGH THEIR WATERY SKY.

"I CHECKED THE TIME. MY AIR WAS ALMOST GONE. I TRIED TO MAKE MY PROBLEM KNOWN TO THEM."

CUT--THE--ROPE!

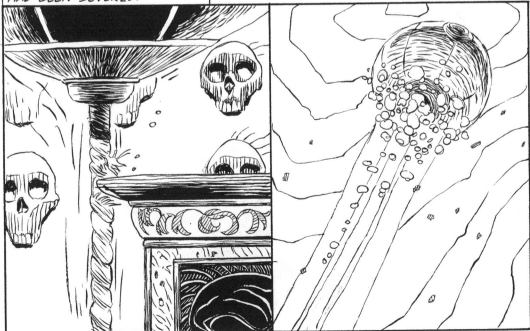

"I BEGAN TO FEEL FAINT. THEN, DIMLY I REALIZED THAT I'D BEEN RELEASED. THE LINE HAD BEEN SEVERED.

"AS TO THE TRIP BACK TO THE SURFACE, I REMEMBER NOTHING. I HAD PASSED OUT."

"AND THE NEXT THING I RECALL, I WAS BACK IN MY CABIN ON THE SOUTHERN STAR."

ALL THAT REMAINS TO BE SAID IS THAT ON FEBRUARY 5, ELSTEAD MADE HIS SECOND DESCENT INTO THE OCEAN ABYSS.

WHAT HAPPENED THEN, WE SHALL NEVER KNOW. FOR HE HAS NEVER RETURNED. PERHAPS HE WAS MADE A CHIEFTAIN OF THE STRANGE CREATURES, AND GIVEN A PLACE OF HONOR IN THEIR UNDERSEA WORLD.

The Truth About Pyecraft

edited & illustrated by

M. K. BROWN

Story by H.G. Wells

He sits not a dozen yards away. If I glance over my shoulder I can see him. And if I catch his eye — and usually I catch his eye — it meets me with an expression.

It is mainly an imploring look — and yet with suspicion in it.

Poor old Pyecraft! Great, uneasy jelly of substance! The fattest clubman in London. The man I helped, the man I shielded, and who has requited me by making my club unendurable, absolutely unendurable, with his liquid appeal, with the perpetual "don't tell" of his looks.

Well, here goes for the truth, the whole truth, and nothing but the truth!

Pyecraft —. I made the acquaintance of Pyecraft in this very smoking-room. I was a young, nervous new member, and he saw it. I was sitting all alone, wishing I knew more of the members, and suddenly he came, a great rolling front of chins and abdomina, towards me, and grunted and sat down in a chair close by me and wheezed for a space, and scraped for a

space with a match and lit a cigar, and then addressed me. I forget what he said — something about the matches not lighting properly, and afterwards as he talked he kept stopping the waiters one by one as they went by, and telling them about the matches in that thin, fluty voice he has. But, anyhow, it was in some such way we began our talking.

"I expect," he said, "you take no more exercise than I do, and probably you eat no less." (Like all excessively obese people he fancied he ate nothing.) "Yet," —and he smiled an oblique smile— "we differ."

And then he began to talk about his fatness and his fatness; all he did for his fatness and all he was going to do for his fatness; what people had advised him to do for his fatness and what he had heard of people doing for fatness similar to his. *A priori*," he said, "one would think a question of nutrition could be answered by dietary and a question of assimilation by drugs." It was stifling. It was dumpling talk. It made me feel swelled to hear him.

One stands that sort of thing once in a way at a club, but a time came when I fancied I was standing too much. He took to me altogether too conspicuously. I could never go into the smoking-room but he would come wallowing towards me, and sometimes he came and gormandised round and about me while I had my lunch. He seemed at times almost to be clinging to me. He was a bore, but not so fearful a bore as to be limited to me; and from the first there was something in his manner—almost as though he knew, almost as though he penetrated to the fact that *I might*—that there was a remote, exceptional chance in me that no one else presented.

"I'd give anything to get it down," he would say—"anything," and peer at

me over his vast cheeks and pant.

Poor old Pyecraft! He has just gonged, no doubt to order another buttered tea-cake!

He came to the actual thing one day. "Our Pharmacopoeia," he said, "our Western Pharmacopoeia, is anything but the last word of medical science. In the East, I've been told—"

He stopped and stared at me. It was like being at an aquarium.

I was quite suddenly angry with him. "Look here," I said, "who told you about my great-grandmother's recipes?"

"Well," he fenced.

"Every time we've met for a week," I said, "and we've met pretty often—you've given me a broad hint or so about that little secret of mine."

"Well," he said, "now the cat's out of the bag, I'll admit, yes, it is so. I had it—"

"From Pattison?"

"Indirectly," he said, which I believe was lying, "yes."

"Pattison," I said, "took that stuff at his own risk."

He pursed his mouth and bowed.

"My great-grandmother's recipes," I said, "are queer things to handle. My father was near making me promise—"

"He didn't?"

"No. But he warned me. He himself used one—once."

"Ah!... But do you think—? Suppose — suppose there did happen to be one—"

"The things are curious documents," I said.

"Even the smell of 'em... No!"

But after going so far Pyecraft was resolved I should go farther. I was always a little afraid if I tried his patience too much he would fall on me suddenly and smother me. I own I was weak. But I was also annoyed with Pyecraft. I had got to that state of feeling for him that disposed me to say, "Well, *take* the risk!" The little affair of Pattison to which I have alluded was a different matter altogether. What it was doesn't concern us now, but I knew, anyhow, that the particular recipe I used then was safe. The rest I didn't know so much about, and, on the whole, I was inclined to doubt their safety pretty completely.

Yet even if Pyecraft got poisoned—

I must confess the poisoning of Pyecraft struck me as an immense undertaking.

That evening I took that queer, odd-scented sandalwood box out of my safe and turned the rustling skins over. The gentleman who wrote the recipes for my great-grandmother evidently had a weakness for skins of a miscellaneous origin, and his handwriting was cramped to the last degree. Some of the things are quite unreadable to me — though my family, with its Indian Civil Service associations, has kept up a knowledge of Hindustani from generation to generation — and none are absolutely plain sailing. But I found the one that I knew was there soon enough, and sat on the floor by my safe for some time looking at it.

"Look here," said I to Pyecraft next day, and snatched the slip away from his eager grasp.

"So far as I — can make it out, this is a recipe for Loss of Weight. ("Ah!" said Pyecraft.) I'm not absolutely sure, but I think it's that. And if you take my advice you'll leave it alone. Because, you know — I blacken my blood in your interest, Pyecraft — my ancestors on that side were, so far as I can gather, a jolly queer lot. See?"

"Let me try it," said Pyecraft.

I leant back in my chair. My imagination made one mighty effort and fell flat within me. "What in Heaven's name, Pyecraft," I asked, "do you think you'll look like when you get thin?"

He was impervious to reason. I made him promise never to say a word to me about his disgusting fatness again whatever happened — never, and then I handed him that little piece of skin.

"It's nasty stuff," I said.

"No matter," he said, and took it.

He goggled at it. "But — but —" he said.

He had just discovered that it wasn't English.

"To the best of my ability," I said, "I will do you a translation."

I did my best. After that we didn't speak for a fortnight. Whenever he approached me I frowned and motioned him away, and he respected our compact, but at the end of a fortnight he was as fat as ever. And then he got a word in.

"I must speak," he said. "It isn't fair. There's something wrong. It's done me no good. You're not doing your great-grandmother justice."

"Where's the recipe?"

He produced it gingerly from his pocketbook.

I ran my eye over the items. "Was the egg addled?" I asked.

"No. Ought it to have been?"

"That," I said, "goes without saying in all my poor dear great-grandmother's recipes. When condition or quality is not specified you must get the worst. She was drastic or nothing... And there's one or two possible alternatives to some of these other things. You got *fresh* rattlesnake venom."

"I got a rattlesnake from Jamrach's. It cost — it cost —"

"That's your affair, anyhow. This last item —"

"I know a man who —"

"Yes. H'm. Well, I'll write the alternatives down. So far as I know the language, the spelling of this recipe is particularly atrocious. By the by, dog here probably means pariah dog."

For a month after that I saw Pyecraft constantly at the club and as fat and anxious as ever. He kept our treaty, but at times he broke the spirit of it by shaking his head despondently. And then, quite unexpectedly, his telegram came.

"Mr. Formalyn!" bawled a page-boy under my nose, and I took the telegram and opened it at once.

"For Heaven's sake come. — Pyecraft."

"H'm," said I, and to tell the truth I was so pleased at the rehabilitation of my great-grandmother's reputation this evidently promised that I made a most excellent lunch.

I got Pyecraft's address from the hall porter. Pyecraft inhabited the upper half of a house in Bloomsbury, and I went there so soon as I had done my coffee and Trappistine. I did not wait to finish my cigar.

"Mr. Pyecraft?" said I, at the front door.

They believed he was ill; he hadn't been out for two days.

"He expects me," said I, and they sent me up.

I rang the bell at the lattice-door upon the landing.

"He shouldn't have tried it, anyhow," I said to myself. "A man who eats like a pig ought to look like a pig."

An obviously worthy woman, with an anxious face and a carelessly placed cap, came and surveyed me through the lattice.

I gave my name and she let me in in a dubious fashion.

"Well?" said I, as we stood together inside Pyecraft's piece of the landing.

"'E said you was to come in if you came," she said, and regarded me, making no motion to show me anywhere. And then, confidentially, "'E's locked in, sir."

"Locked in?"

"Locked himself in yesterday morning and 'asn't let any one in since, sir. And ever and again *swearing*. Oh, my!"

I stared at the door she indicated by her glances.

"In there?" I said.

"Yes, sir."

"What's up?"

She shook her head sadly, "'E keeps on calling for vittles, sir. *'Eavy* vittles 'e wants. I get 'im what I can. Pork 'e's 'ad, sooit puddin', sossiges, noo bread. Left outside, if you please, and me go away. 'E's eatin', sir, somethink *awful*."

There came a piping bawl from inside the door: "That Formalyn?"

"That you, Pyecraft?" I shouted, and went and banged the door.

"Tell her to go away."

I did.

Then I could hear a curious pattering upon the door, almost like some one feeling for the handle in the dark, and Pyecraft's familiar grunts.

"It's all right," I said, "she's gone."

But for a long time the door didn't open.

I heard the key turn. Then Pyecraft's voice said, "Come in."

I turned the handle and opened the door. Naturally I expected to see Pyecraft.

Well, you know, he wasn't there!

I never had such a shock in my life. There was his sitting-room in a state of untidy disorder, plates and dishes among the books and writing things, and several chairs overturned, but Pyecraft —

"It's all right, o' man; shut the door," he said, and then I discovered him.

There he was right up close to the cornice in the corner by the door, as though some one had glued him to the ceiling. His face was anxious and angry. He panted and gesticulated. "Shut the door," he said. "If that woman gets hold of it —"

I shut the door, and went and stood away from him and stared.

"If anything gives way and you tumble down," I said, "you'll break your neck, Pyecraft."

"I wish I could," he wheezed.

"A man of your age and weight getting up to kiddish gymnastics —"

"Don't," he said, and looked agonised.

"I'll tell you," he said, and gesticulated.

"How the deuce," said I, "are you holding on up there?"

And then abruptly I realised that he was not holding on at all, that he was floating up there—just as a gas-filled bladder might have floated in the same position. He began a struggle to thrust himself away from the ceiling and to clamber down the wall to me. "It's that prescription," he panted, as he did so. "Your great-gran—"

He took hold of a framed engraving rather carelessly as he spoke and it gave way, and he flew back to the ceiling again, while the picture smashed onto the sofa. Bump he went against the ceiling, and I knew then why he was all over white on the more salient curves and angles of his person. He tried again more carefully, coming down by way of the mantel.

It was really a most extraordinary spectacle, that great, fat, apoplectic-looking man upside down and trying to get from the ceiling to the floor. "That prescription," he said. "Too successful."

"How?"

"Loss of weight—almost complete."

And then, of course, I understood.

"By Jove, Pyecraft," said I, "what you wanted was a cure for fatness! But you always called it weight. You would call it weight."

Somehow I was extremely delighted. I quite liked Pyecraft for the time. "Let me help you!" I said, and took his hand and pulled him down. He kicked about, trying to get a foothold somewhere. It was very like holding a flag on a windy day.

"That table," he said, pointing, "is solid mahogany and very heavy. If you can put me under that—"

I did, and there he wallowed about like a captive balloon, while I stood on his hearthrug and talked to him.

I lit a cigar. "Tell me," I said, "what happened?"

"I took it," he said.

"How did it taste?"

"Oh, *beastly!*"

I should fancy they all did. Whether one regards the ingredients or the probable compound or the possible results, almost all of my great-grandmother's remedies appear to me at least to be extraordinarily uninviting. For my own part—

"I took a little sip first."

"Yes?"

"And as I felt lighter and better after an hour, I decided to take the draught."

"My dear Pyecraft!"

"I held my nose," he explained. "And then I kept on getting lighter and lighter—and helpless, you know."

He gave way to a sudden burst of passion. "What the goodness am I to *do?*" he said.

"There's one thing pretty evident," I said, "that you mustn't do. If you go out of doors, you'll go up and up." I waved an arm upward. "They'd have to send Santos-Dumont after you to bring you down again."

"I suppose it will wear off?"

I shook my head. "I don't think you can count on that," I said.

And then there was another burst of passion, and he kicked out at adjacent chairs and banged the floor. He behaved just as I should have expected a great, fat, self-indulgent man to behave under trying circumstances—that is to say, very badly. He spoke of me and my great-grandmother with an utter want of discretion.

"I never asked you to take the stuff," I said.

And generously disregarding the insults he was putting upon me, I sat down in his armchair and began to talk to him in a sober, friendly fashion.

I pointed out to him that this was a trouble he had brought upon himself, and that it had almost an air of poetical justice. He had eaten too much. This he disputed, and for a time we argued the point.

He became noisy and violent, so I desisted from this aspect of his lesson. "And then," said I, "you committed the sin of euphuism. You called it not Fat, which is just and inglorious, but Weight. You—"

He interrupted to say he recognised all that. What was he to *do*?

I suggested he should adapt himself to his new conditions. So we came to the really sensible part of the business. I suggested that it would not be difficult for him to learn to walk about on the ceiling with his hands—

"I can't sleep," he said.

But that was no great difficulty. It was quite possible, I pointed out, to make a shake-up under a wire mattress, fasten the under things on with tapes, and have a blanket, sheet, and coverlet to button at the side. He would have to confide in his housekeeper, I said; and after some squabbling he agreed to that. (Afterwards it was quite delightful to see the beautifully matter-of-fact way with which the good lady took all these amazing inversions.) He could have a library ladder in his room, and all his meals could be laid on the top of his bookcase. We also hit on an ingenious device by which he could get to the floor whenever he wanted, which was simply to put the *British Encyclopaedia* (tenth edition) on the top of his open shelves. He just pulled out a couple of volumes and held on, and down he came. And we agreed there must be iron staples along the skirting, so that he could cling to those whenever he wanted to get about the room on the lower level.

As we got on with the thing I found myself almost keenly interested. It was I who called in the housekeeper and broke matters to her, and it was I chiefly who fixed up the inverted bed. In fact, I spent two whole days at his flat. I am a handy, interfering sort of man with a screwdriver, and I made all sorts of ingenious adaptations for him — ran a wire to bring his bells within reach, turned all his electric lights up instead of down, and so on. The whole affair was extremely curious and interesting to me, and it was delightful to think of Pyecraft like some great, fat blow-fly, crawling about on his ceiling and clambering round the lintels of his doors from one room to another, and never, never, never coming to the club any more...

Then, you know, my fatal ingenuity got the better of me. I was sitting by his fire drinking his whisky, and he was up in his favourite corner by the cornice, tacking a Turkey carpet to the ceiling, when the idea struck me. "By Jove, Pyecraft!" I said, "all this is totally unnecessary."

84

And before I could calculate the complete consequences of my notion I blurted it out. "Lead underclothing," said I, and the mischief was done.

Pyecraft received the thing almost in tears. "To be right ways up again —" he said. I gave him the whole secret before I saw where it would take me. "Buy sheet lead," I said, "stamp it into discs. Sew 'em all over your underclothes until you have enough. Have lead-soled boots, carry a bag of solid lead, and the thing is done! Instead of being a prisoner here you may go abroad again, Pyecraft; you may travel —"

A still happier idea came to me. "You need never fear a shipwreck. All you need do is just slip off some or all of your clothes, take the necessary amount of luggage in your hand, and float up in the air —"

In his emotion he dropped the tack-hammer within an ace of my head. "By Jove!" he said, "I shall be able to come back to the club again."

The thing pulled me up short. "By Jove!" I said faintly. "Yes. Of course — you will."

He did. He does. There he sits behind me now, stuffing — as I live! — a third go of buttered tea-cake. And no one in the whole world knows — except his housekeeper and me — that he weighs practically nothing; that he is a mere boring mass of assimilatory matter, mere clouds in clothing, *niente*, *nefas*, the most inconsiderable of men. There he sits watching until I have done this writing. Then, if he can, he will waylay me. He will come billowing up to me...

He will tell me over again all about it, how it feels, how it doesn't feel, how he sometimes hopes it is passing off a little. And always somewhere in that fat, abundant discourse he will say, "The secret's keeping, eh? If any one knew of it — I should be so ashamed... Makes a fellow look such a fool, you know. Crawling about on a ceiling and all that..."

And now to elude Pyecraft, occupying, as he does, an admirable strategic position between me and the door. ✒

THE TIME MACHINE

a portfolio of illustrations by

NICOLA CUTI

©2002 NICOLA CUTI

*With excerpts from the story
by H.G. Wells*

"This little affair," said the Time Traveller, "is only a model. It is my plan for a machine to travel through time. Now I want you clearly to understand that this lever, being pressed over, sends the machine gliding into the future, and this other reverses the motion. Presently I am going to press the lever, and off the machine will go. It will vanish, pass into future time, and disappear."

"I drew a breath, set my teeth, gripped the starting lever with both hands, and went off with a thud. The dim suggestion of the laboratory seemed presently to fall away from me, and I saw the sun hopping swiftly across the sky, leaping it every minute, and every minute marking a day. With a kind of madness growing upon me, I flung myself into futurity."

"In another moment we were standing face to face, I and this fragile thing out of futurity. He came straight up to me and laughed into my eyes. The absence from his bearing of any sign of fear struck me at once. There was something in these pretty little people that inspired confidence — a graceful gentleness, a certain childlike ease."

"The building had a huge entry, and was altogether of colossal dimensions. The big doorway opened into a proportionately great hall hung with brown. Perhaps the thing that struck me most was its dilapidated look. The stained-glass windows, which displayed only a geometrical pattern, were broken in many places, and the curtains that hung across the lower end were thick with dust."

"As I was watching some of the little people bathing in a shallow, one of them was seized with cramp and began drifting downstream. None of these creatures made the slightest attempt to rescue the weakly crying little thing which was drowning before their eyes. When I realized this, I hurriedly slipped off my clothes, and, wading in, caught the poor mite and drew her safe to land."

"Presently the walls fell away from me, and I came to a large open space. Striking another match,
I saw that I had entered a vast arched cavern which stretched into utter darkness beyond the range
of my light. Great shapes like big machines rose out of the dimness and cast grotesque black
shadows in which dim, spectral Morlocks sheltered from the glare."

"I observed far off, a vast green structure, different in character from any I had hitherto seen. It was larger than the largest of the palaces or ruins I knew, and the façade had an Oriental look, as well as the pale-green tint of Chinese porcelain. I was minded to push on and explore. Taking Weena like a child upon my shoulder, I went up the hills towards the palace."

"Looking back, I saw, through the black pillars of the nearer trees, the flames of the burning forest. The whole space was as bright as day with the reflection of the fire. Upon the hillside were some thirty or forty Morlocks, dazzled by the light and heat, and blundering hither and thither against each other in their bewilderment."

"Above me towered the sphinx upon the bronze pedestal, white, shining, leprous, in the light of the rising moon. It seemed to smile in mockery of my dismay. And now came a most unexpected thing. As I approached the pedestal of the sphinx I found the bronze valves were open. Within was a small apartment, and on a raised place in the corner of this was the Time Machine."

"I saw that what I had taken to be a reddish mass of rock was moving slowly towards me. Then I saw the thing was really a monstrous crab-like creature. Its evil eyes were wriggling on their stalks, its mouth was all alive with appetite, and its vast claws were descending upon me. In a moment my hand was on the lever, and I had placed a month between myself and these monsters."

The Temptation of Harringay

illustrated by

MILTON KNIGHT

Story by H.G. Wells

It is quite impossible to say whether this thing really happened. It depends entirely on the word of R. M. Harringay, who is an artist.

Following his version of the affair, the narrative deposes that Harringay went into his studio about ten o'clock to see what he could make of the head that he had been working at the day before. The head in question was that of an Italian organ-grinder, and Harringay thought—but was not quite sure—that the title would be the "Vigil." So far he is frank, and his narrative bears the stamp of truth. He had seen the man expectant for pennies, and with a promptness that suggested genius, had had him in at once.

"Kneel. Look up at that bracket," said Harringay. "As if you expected pennies.

"Don't *grin!*" said Harringay. "I don't want to paint your gums. Look as though you were unhappy."

Now, after a night's rest, the picture proved decidedly unsatisfactory. "It's good work," said Harringay. "That little bit in the neck... But."

He walked about the studio, and looked at the thing from this point and from that. Then he said a wicked word. In the original the word is given.

"Painting," he says he said. "Just a painting of an organ-grinder—a mere portrait. If it was a live organ-grinder I wouldn't mind. But somehow I never make things alive. I wonder if my imagination is wrong."

This, too, has a truthful air. His imagination *is* wrong.

"That creative touch! To take canvas and pigment and make a man—as Adam was made of red ochre! But this thing! If you met it walking about the streets you would know it was only a studio

©2002 MILTON KNIGHT

production. The little boys would tell it to 'Garnome and git frimed.' Some little touch... Well—it won't do as it is."

He went to the blinds and began to pull them down. They were made of blue holland with the rollers at the bottom of the window, so that you pull them down to get more light. He gathered his palette, brushes, and mahl stick from his table. Then he turned to the picture and put a speck of brown in the corner of the mouth; and shifted his attention thence to the pupil of the eye. Then he decided that the chin was a trifle too impassive for a vigil.

Presently he put down his impedimenta, and lighting a pipe surveyed the progress of his work. "I'm hanged if the thing isn't sneering at me," said Harringay, and he still believes it sneered.

The animation of the figure had certainly increased, but scarcely in the direction he wished. There was no mistake about the sneer. "Vigil of the Unbeliever," said Harringay. "Rather subtle and clever that! But the left eyebrow isn't cynical enough."

He went and dabbed at the eyebrow, and added a little to the lobe of the ear to suggest materialism. Further consideration ensued. "Vigil's off, I'm afraid," said Harringay. "Why not Mephistopheles? But that's a bit *too* common. 'A Friend of the Doge'—not so seedy. The armour won't do, though, Too Camelot. How about a scarlet robe and call him 'One of the Sacred College'? Humour in that, and an appreciation of Middle Italian History.

"There's always Benvenuto Cellini," said Harringay; "with a clever suggestion of a gold cup in one corner. But that would scarcely suit the complexion."

He describes himself as babbling in this way in order to keep down an unaccountably unpleasant sensation of fear. The thing was certainly acquiring anything but a pleasing expression. Yet it was as certainly becoming far more of a living thing than it had been—if a sinister one—far more alive than anything he had ever painted before. "Call it 'Portrait of a Gentleman,'" said Harringay; "A Certain Gentleman."

"Won't do," said Harringay, still

keeping up his courage. "Kind of thing they call Bad Taste. That sneer will have to come out. That gone, and a little more fire in the eye—never noticed how warm his eye was before—and he might do for—? What price Passionate Pilgrim? But that devilish face won't do—*this* side of the Channel.

"Some little inaccuracy does it," he said; "eyebrows probably too oblique"—therewith pulling the blind lower to get a better light, and resuming palette and brushes.

The face on the canvas seemed animated by a spirit of its own. Where the expression of diablerie came in he found impossible to discover. Experiment was necessary. The eyebrows—it could scarcely be the eyebrows? But he altered them. No, that was no better; in fact, if anything, a trifle more satanic. The cor-

ner of the mouth? Pah! more than ever a leer—and now, retouched, it was ominously grim. The eye, then? Catastrophe! he had filled his brush with vermilion instead of brown, and yet he had felt sure it was brown! The eye seemed now to have rolled in its socket, and was glaring at him an eye of fire. In a flash of passion, possibly with something of the courage of panic, he struck the brush full of bright red athwart the picture; and then a very curious thing, a very strange thing indeed, occurred—if it *did* occur.

The diabolified Italian before him shut both his eyes, pursed his mouth, and wiped the colour off his face with his hand.

Then the *red eye* opened again, with a sound like the opening of lips, and the face smiled. "That was rather hasty of you," said the picture.

Harringay states that, now that the worst had happened, his self-possession returned. He had a saving persuasion that devils were reasonable creatures.

"Why do you keep moving about then," he said, "making faces and all that—sneering and squinting, while I am painting you?"

"I don't," said the picture.

"You *do*," said Harringay.

"It's yourself," said the picture.

"It's *not* myself," said Harringay.

"It *is* yourself," said the picture. "No! don't go hitting me with paint again, because it's true. You have been trying to fluke an expression on my face all the morning. Really, you haven't an idea what your picture ought to look like."

"I have," said Harringay.

"You have *not*," said the picture: "You *never* have with your pictures. You always start with the vaguest presentiment of what you are going to do; it is to be

something beautiful—you are sure of that—and devout, perhaps, or tragic; but beyond that it is all experiment and chance. My dear fellow! you don't think you can paint a picture like that?"

Now it must be remembered that for what follows we have only Harringay's word.

"I shall paint a picture exactly as I like," said Harringay, calmly.

This seemed to disconcert the picture a little. "You can't paint a picture without an inspiration," it remarked.

"But I *had* an inspiration—for this."

"Inspiration!" sneered the sardonic figure; "a fancy that came from your seeing an organ-grinder looking up at a window! Vigil! Ha, ha! You just started painting on the chance of something coming—that's what you did. And when I saw you at it I came. I want a talk with you!

"Art, with you," said the picture—"it's a poor business. You potter. I don't know

101

how it is, but you don't seem able to throw your soul into it. You know too much. It hampers you. In the midst of your enthusiasms you ask yourself whether something like this has not been done before. And..."

"Look here," said Harringay, who had expected something better than criticism from the devil. "Are you going to talk studio to me?" He filled his number twelve hoghair with red paint.

"The true artist," said the picture, "is always an ignorant man. An artist who theorises about his work is no longer artist but critic. Wagner...I say!—What's that red paint for?"

"I'm going to paint you out," said Harringay. "I don't want to hear all that Tommy Rot. If you think just because I'm an artist by trade I'm going to talk studio to you, you make a precious mistake."

"One minute," said the picture, evidently alarmed. "I want to make you an offer—a genuine offer. It's right what I'm saying. You lack inspirations. Well. No doubt you've heard of the Cathedral of Cologne, and the Devil's Bridge, and—"

"Rubbish," said Harringay. "Do you think I want to go to perdition simply for the pleasure of painting a good picture, and getting it slated. Take that."

His blood was up. His danger only nerved him to action, so he says. So he planted a dab of vermilion in his creature's mouth. The Italian spluttered and tried to wipe it off—evidently horribly surprised. And then—according to Harringay—there began a very remarkable struggle, Harringay splashing away with the red paint, and the picture wriggling about and wiping it off as fast as he put it on. "Two masterpieces," said the demon. "Two indubitable masterpieces for a Chelsea artist's soul. It's a bargain?" Harringay replied with the paint brush.

For a few minutes nothing could be heard but the brush going and the spluttering and ejaculations of the Italian. A lot of the strokes he caught on his arm and hand, though Harringay got over his guard often enough. Presently the paint on the palette gave out and the two antagonists stood breathless, regarding each other. The picture was so smeared with red that it looked as if it had been rolling about a slaughterhouse, and it was painfully out of breath and very uncomfortable with the wet paint trickling down its neck. Still, the first round was in its favour on the whole. "Think," it said, sticking pluckily to its point, "two supreme masterpieces—in different styles. Each equivalent to the Cathedral..."

"I know," said Harringay, and rushed out of the studio and along the passage towards his wife's boudoir.

In another minute he was back with a large tin of enamel—Hedge Sparrow's Egg Tint, it was, and a brush. At the sight of that the artistic devil with the red eye began to scream. "*Three* masterpieces-culminating masterpieces."

Harringay delivered cut two across the demon, and followed with a thrust in the eye. There was an indistinct rumbling. "*Four* masterpieces," and a spitting sound.

But Harringay had the upper hand now and meant to keep it. With rapid, bold strokes he continued to paint over the writhing canvas, until at last it was a uniform field of shining Hedge Sparrow tint. Once the mouth reappeared and got as far as "Five master—" before he filled it with enamel; and near the end the red eye opened and glared at him indignantly. But at last nothing remained save a gleaming panel of drying enamel. For a little while a faint stirring beneath the surface puckered it slightly here and there, but presently even that died away and the thing was perfectly still.

Then Harringay — according to Harringay's account—lit his pipe and sat down and stared at the enameled canvas, and tried to make out clearly what had happened. Then he walked round behind it, to see if the back of it was at all remarkable. Then it was he began to regret that he had not photographed the Devil before he painted him out.

This is Harringay's story—not mine. He supports it by a small canvas (24 by 20) enameled a pale green, and by violent asseverations. It is also true that he never has produced a masterpiece, and in the opinion of his intimate friends probably never will. 🌹

THE WAR OF THE WORLDS

The story of Orson Welles' 1938 radio broadcast
written by

ANTONELLA CAPUTO

illustrated by

NICK MILLER

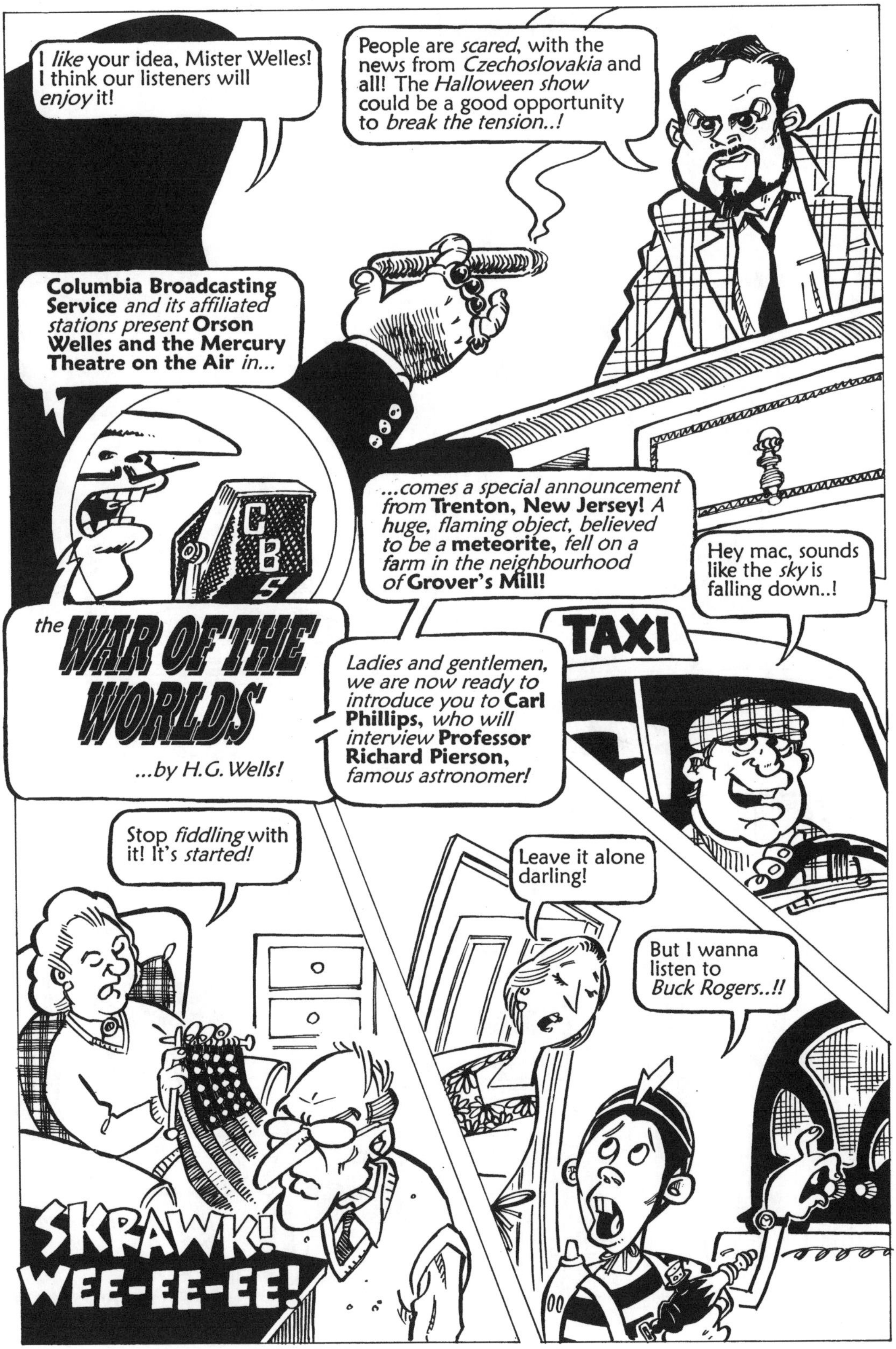
I *like* your idea, Mister Welles! I think our listeners will *enjoy* it!
People are *scared*, with the news from *Czechoslovakia* and **all**! The *Halloween show* could be a good opportunity to *break the tension..!*
Columbia Broadcasting Service *and its affiliated stations present* **Orson Welles and the Mercury Theatre on the Air** *in...*
CBS
...comes a special announcement from **Trenton, New Jersey!** *A huge, flaming object, believed to be a* **meteorite,** *fell on a farm in the neighbourhood of* **Grover's Mill!**
Hey mac, sounds like the *sky* is falling down..!
TAXI
the WAR OF THE WORLDS ...by H.G. Wells!
Ladies and gentlemen, we are now ready to introduce you to **Carl Phillips,** *who will interview* **Professor Richard Pierson,** *famous astronomer!*
Stop *fiddling* with it! It's *started!*
Leave it alone darling!
But I wanna listen to *Buck Rogers..!!*
SKRAWK! WEE-EE-EE!

Ladies and gentlemen, this is **Carl Phillips** at Wilmuth Farm...well, I just got here... yes, I guess that's the ~ the 'thing' right in front of me... what I can see of the object...

...itself doesn't look very much like a meteor... it looks like a **huge cylinder...**What's the diameter, Professor Pierson...?

About thirty yards.

Here's Mister Wilmuth, owner of the farm. Mister Wilmuth, will you please tell the radio audience what happened?

I heard something like a hissing sound... like 'ssssssssssssssss'... I seen a kinda streak and then **ZIGO!** something smacked the ground...

Just a minute! Something's happening! Ladies and Gentlemen, this is terrific! The end of the thing is beginning to flake off! The top is beginning to rotate like a screw..

She's moving!

SCRAPING NOISES

Keep back, there!

It's **red hot,** they'll burn to a cinder...!

STAND BACK!!

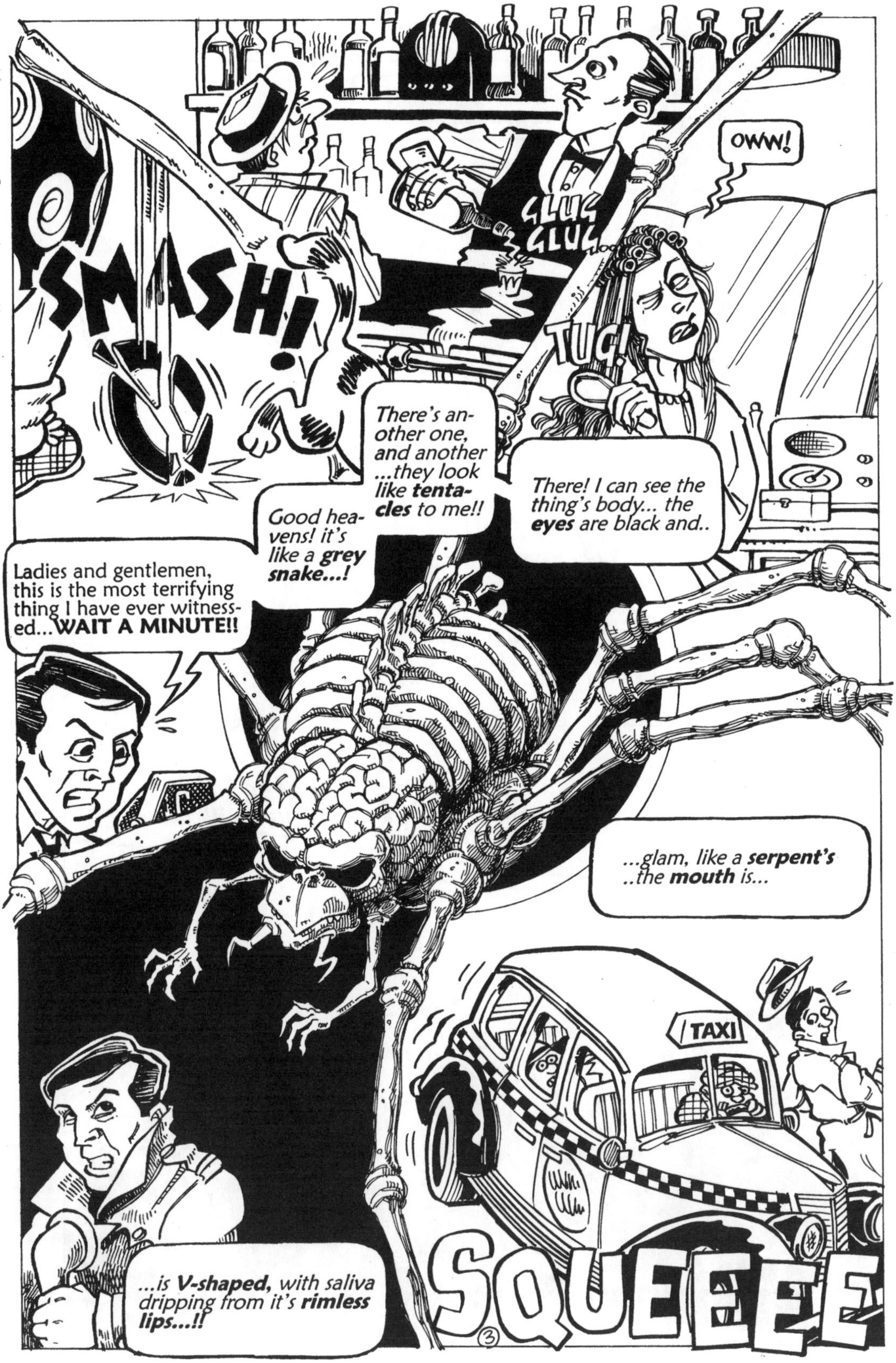
SMASH!
GLUG GLUG
OWW!
TUG!
Ladies and gentlemen, this is the most terrifying thing I have ever witnessed... **WAIT A MINUTE!!**
Good heavens! it's like a **grey snake...!**
There's another one, and another ...they look like **tentacles** to me!!
There! I can see the thing's body... the **eyes** are black and..
...glam, like a **serpent's** ..the **mouth** is...
TAXI
...is **V-shaped,** with saliva dripping from it's **rimless lips...!!**
SQUEEEE

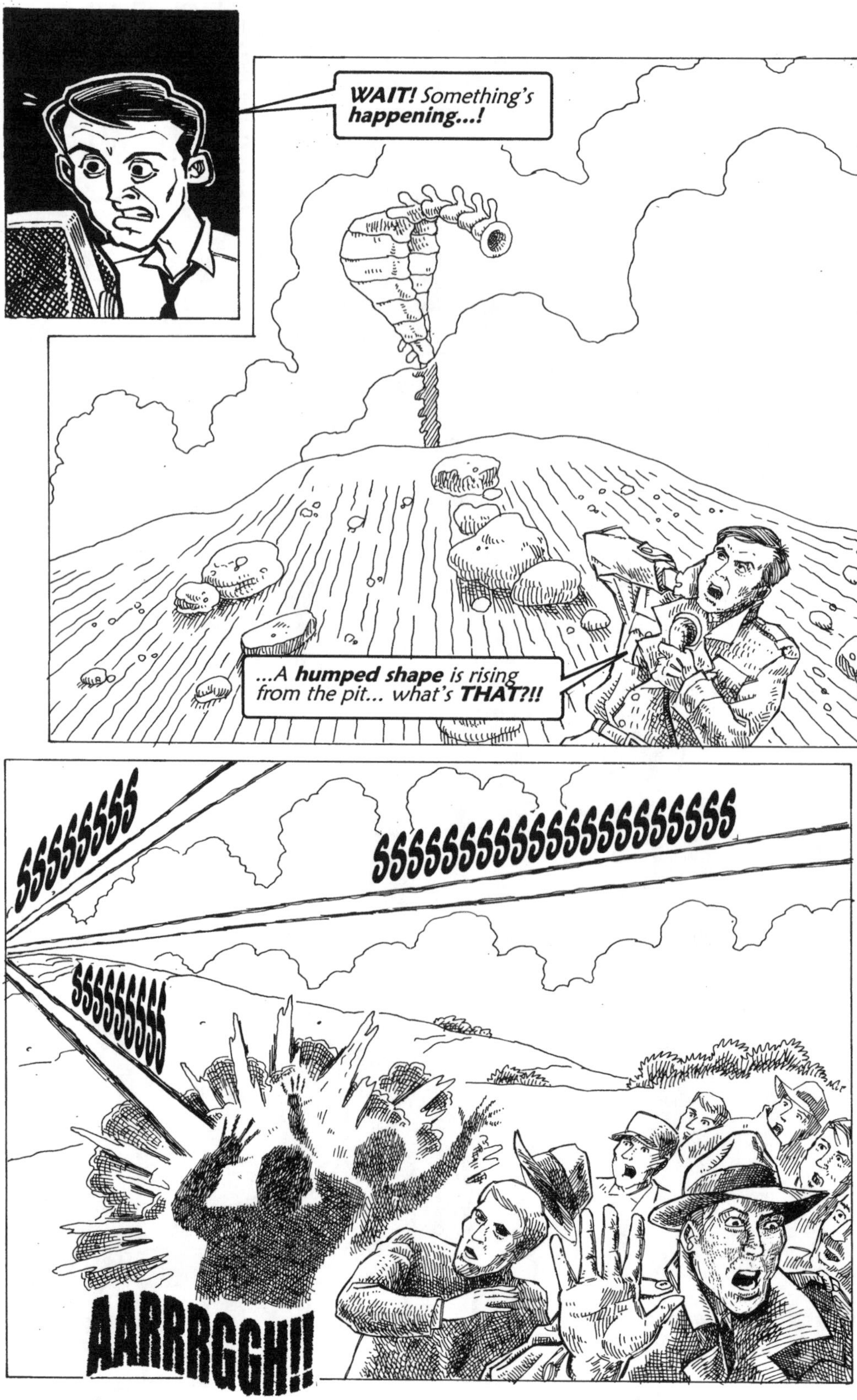
WAIT! Something's happening...!
...A humped shape is rising from the pit... what's THAT?!!
SSSSSSSS
SSSSSSSSSSSSSSSSSSSSSSSS
SSSSSSSSS
AARRRGGH!!

CHAKKA CHAKKA...

Excuse me... what time does the world end...?

to all receivers: station w a b c broadcast is a drama. re: this section being attacked by residents of mars: imaginary affair.

They're bombing New Jersey! I heard it on the radio! Hello...?

The world is coming to an end, and I have a lot to do...!!

109

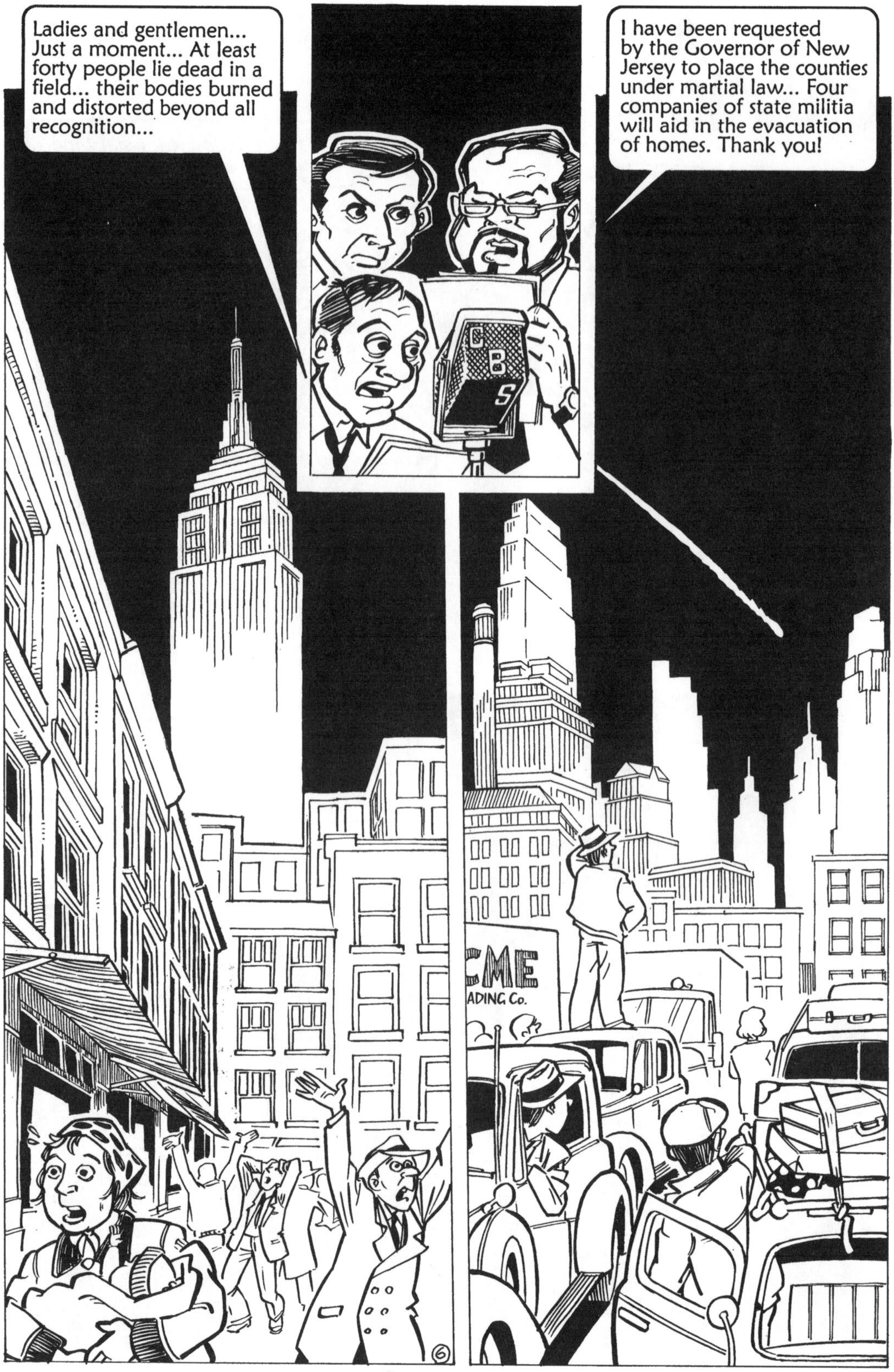
Ladies and gentlemen... Just a moment... At least forty people lie dead in a field... their bodies burned and distorted beyond all recognition...
CBS
I have been requested by the Governor of New Jersey to place the counties under martial law... Four companies of state militia will aid in the evacuation of homes. Thank you!
CME
ADING Co.

I shall refer to the mysterious weapon as a "heat ray". It's all too evident that these creatures have scientific knowledge far in advance of our own!

This is **Captain Lansing** of the **Signal Corps!** Well, we ought to see some action soon! A **quick thrust** and it will all be over... Now ~ **WAIT A MINUTE!** I see something on top of the cylinder...!

Seven thousand men closing in on an old metal tube... *WAIT, THAT WASN'T A SHADOW...!!*

WHY, IT'S STANDING ON LEGS...ACTUALLY REARING UP IN A SORT OF METAL FRAMEWORK...!!!

It's something moving... SOLID METAL... KIND OF A SHIELD-LIKE AFFAIR RISING UP OUT OF THE CYLINDER ...IT'S GOING HIGHER AND HIGHER...

SAM

ACME RADIO
& ELECTRICAL SUPPLY Co.

LISTEN TO THIS!!

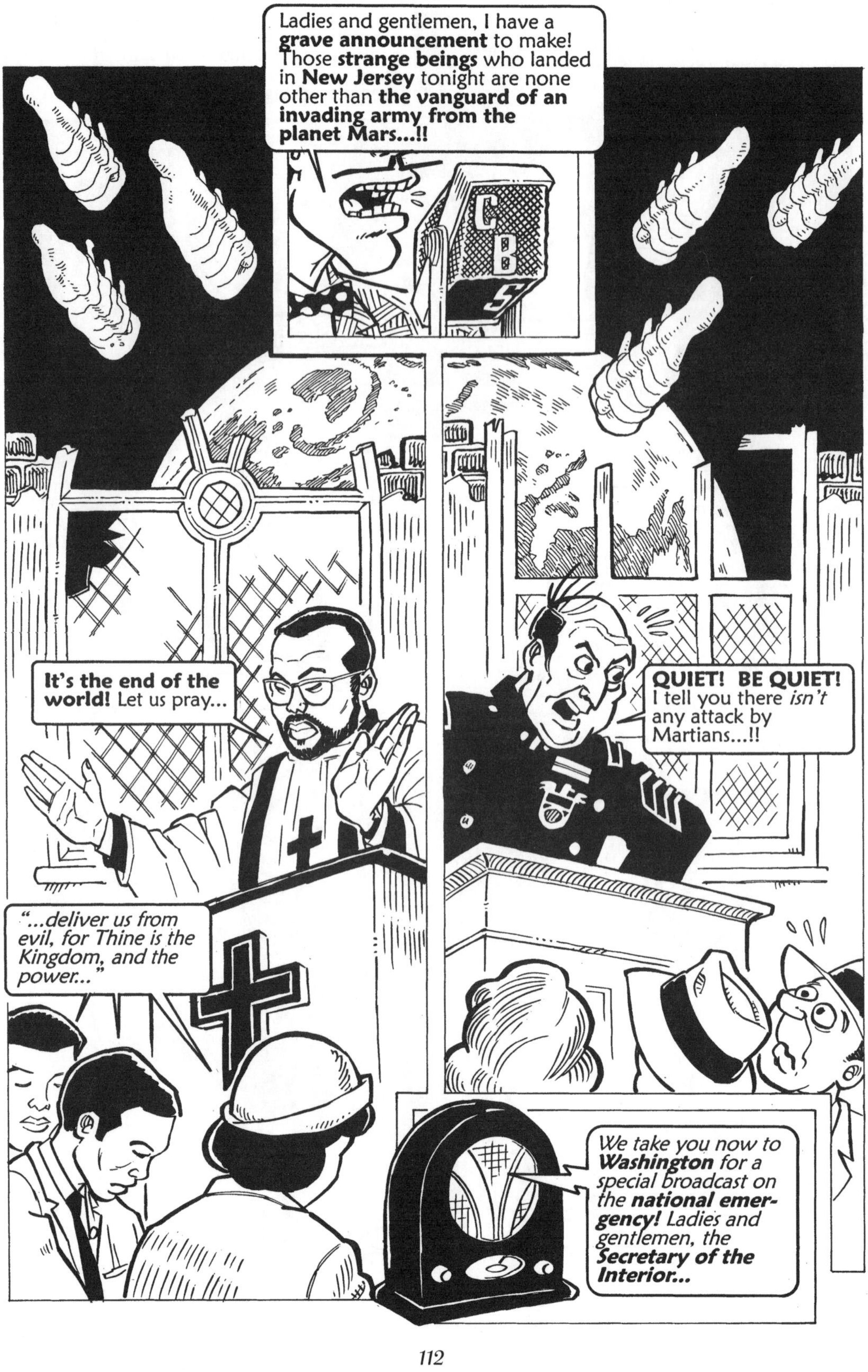
Ladies and gentlemen, I have a **grave announcement** to make! Those **strange beings** who landed in **New Jersey** tonight are none other than **the vanguard of an invading army from the planet Mars...!!**
CBS
It's the end of the world! Let us pray...
QUIET! BE QUIET! I tell you there *isn't* any attack by Martians...!!
"...deliver us from evil, for Thine is the Kingdom, and the power..."
*We take you now to **Washington** for a special broadcast on the **national emergency!** Ladies and gentlemen, the **Secretary of the Interior...***

JOHN HOUSEMAN   MARTIN GABEL

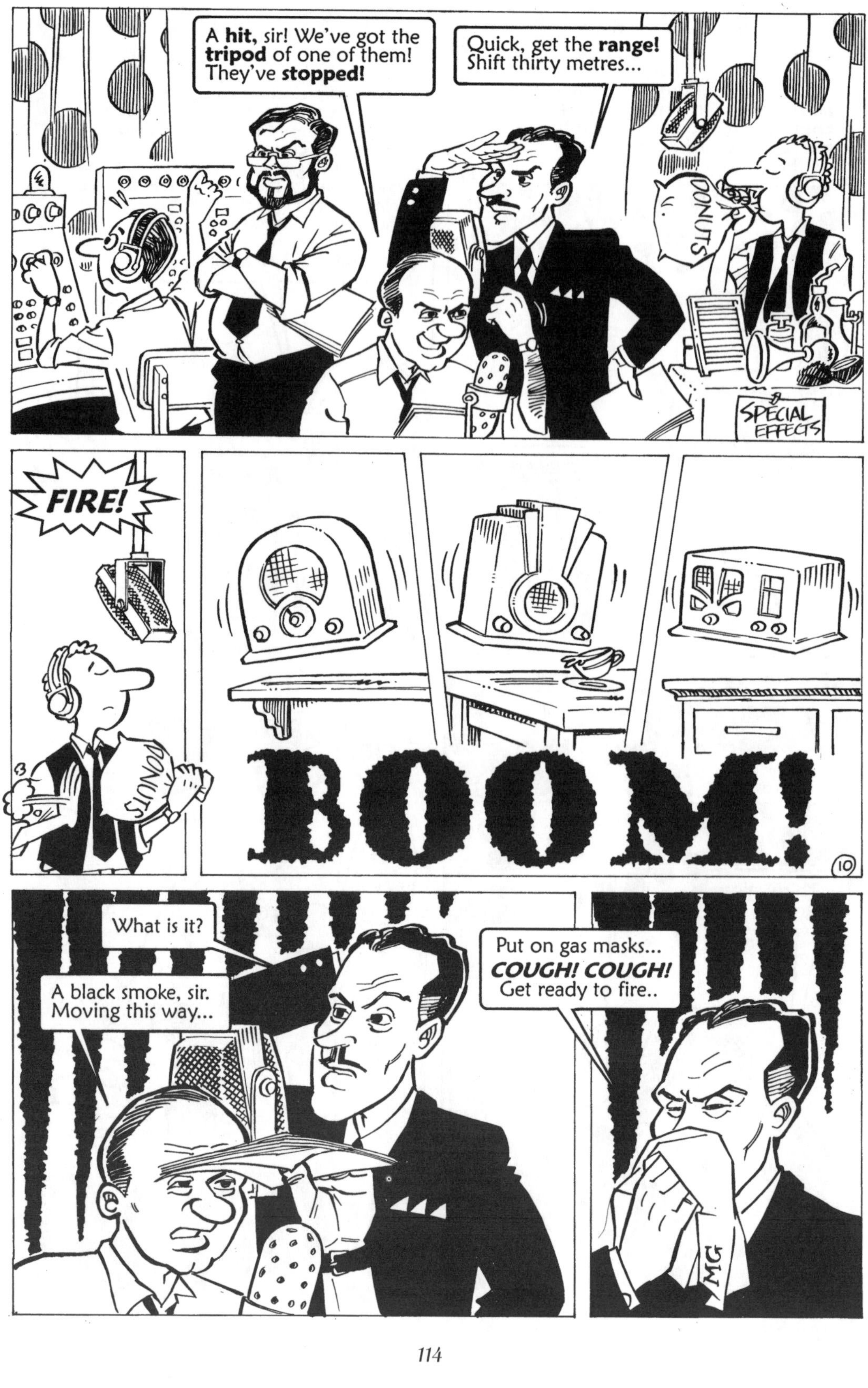
A **hit,** sir! We've got the **tripod** of one of them! They've **stopped!**
Quick, get the **range!** Shift thirty metres...
DONUTS
SPECIAL EFFECTS
FIRE!
DONUTS
BOOM!
10
What is it?
A black smoke, sir. Moving this way...
Put on gas masks... ***COUGH! COUGH!*** Get ready to fire..
MG

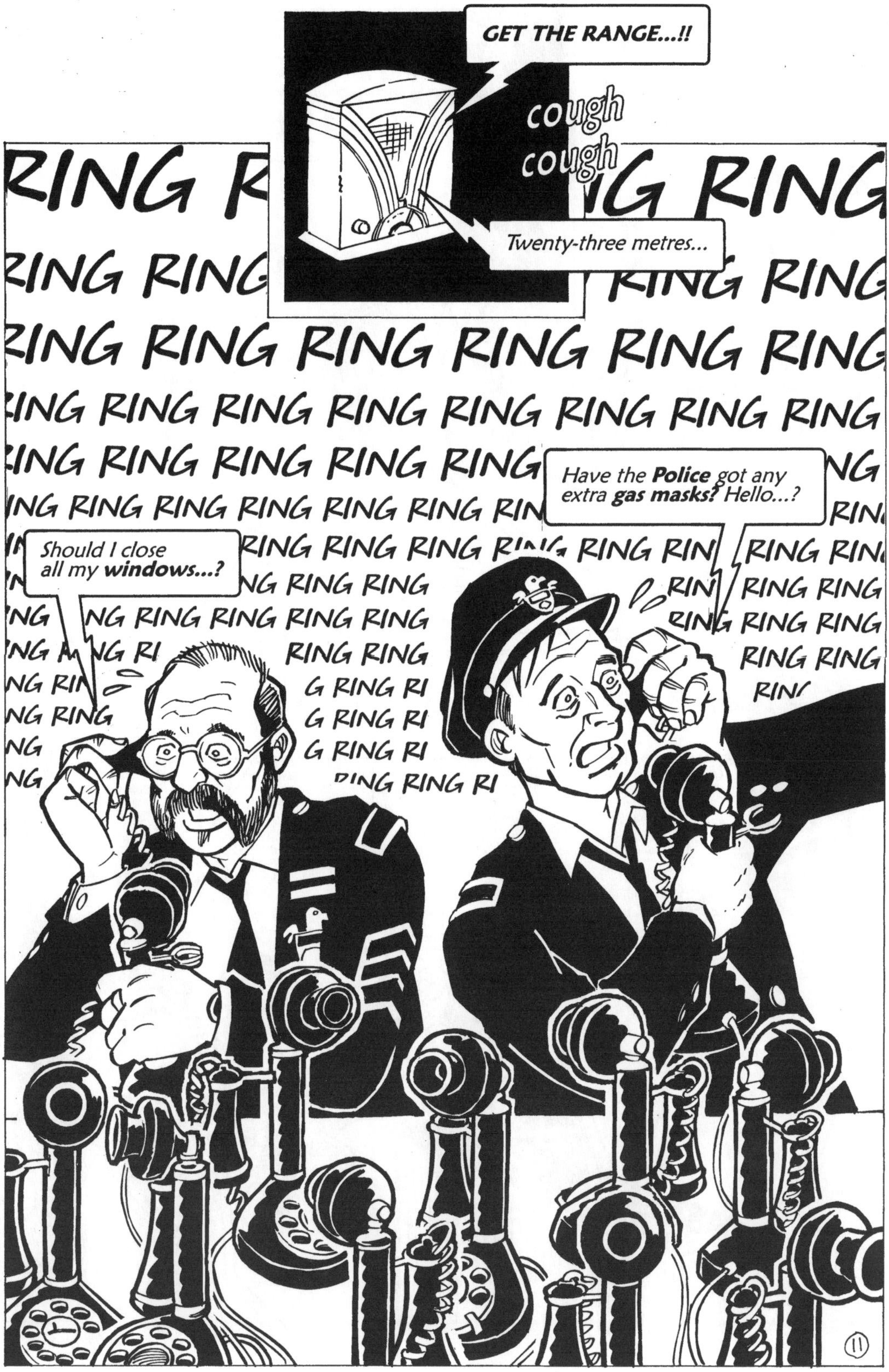
GET THE RANGE...!!
cough cough
Twenty-three metres...
RING RING RING RING RING RING
Should I close all my **windows**...?
Have the **Police** got any extra **gas masks?** Hello...?

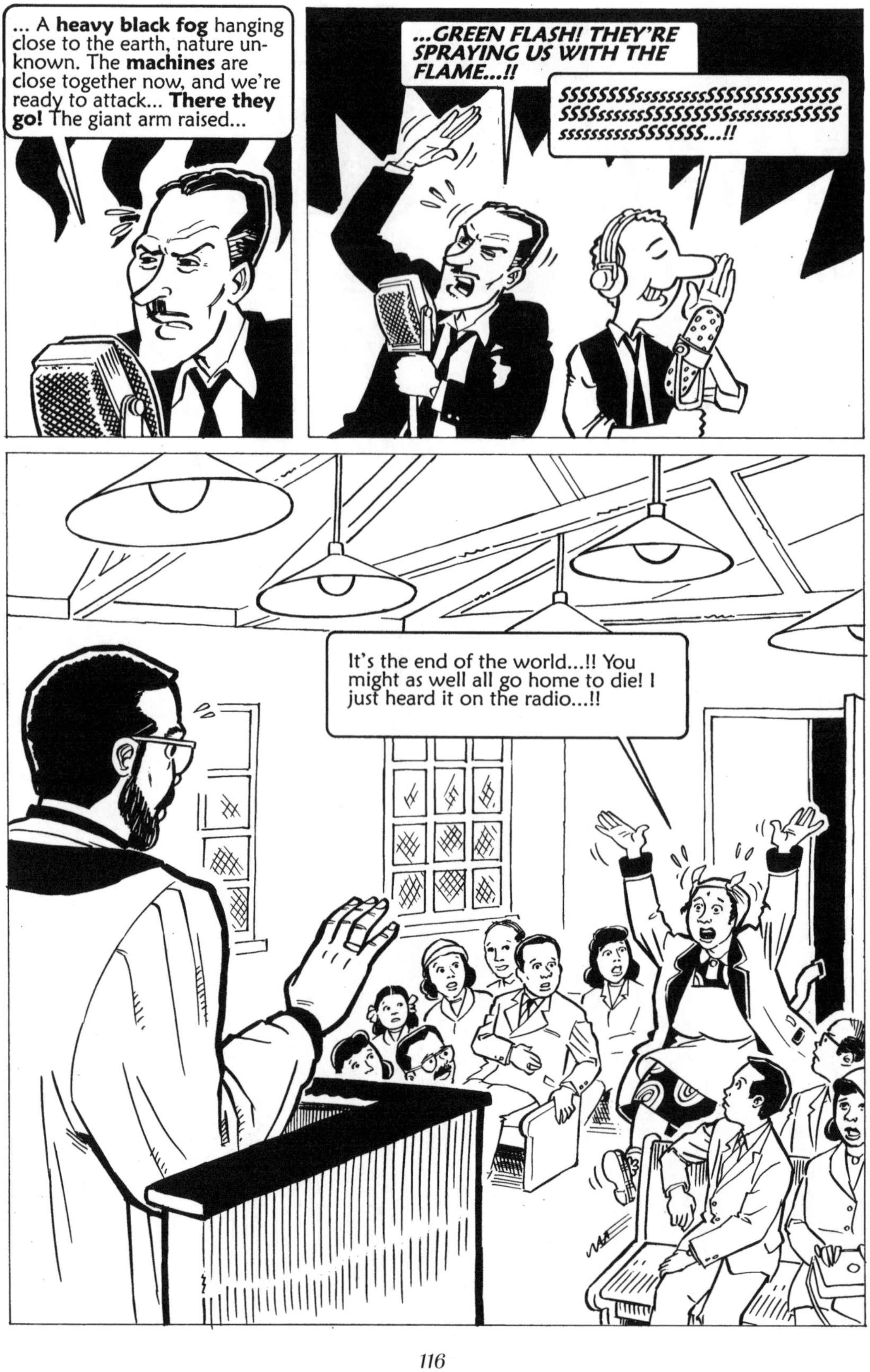
... A **heavy black fog** hanging close to the earth, nature unknown. The **machines** are close together now, and we're ready to attack... **There they go!** The giant arm raised...
...GREEN FLASH! THEY'RE SPRAYING US WITH THE FLAME...!!
SSSSSSSSssssssssSSSSSSSSSSSSSS SSSSsssssSSSSSSSSSssssssssSSSSS ssssssssssSSSSSSS...!!
It's the end of the world...!! You might as well all go home to die! I just heard it on the radio...!!

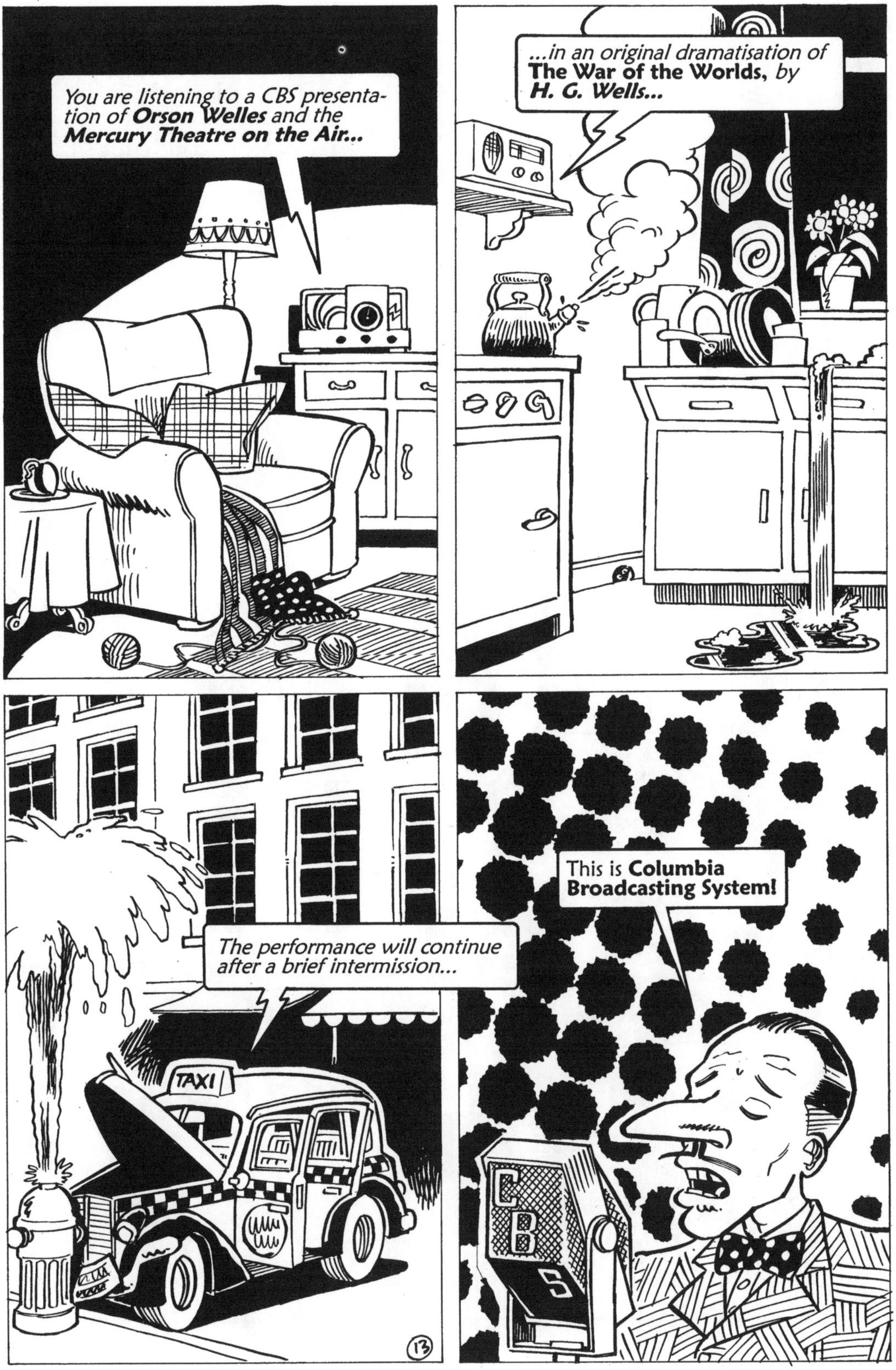
You are listening to a CBS presentation of **Orson Welles** and the **Mercury Theatre on the Air...**
...in an original dramatisation of **The War of the Worlds,** *by* **H. G. Wells...**
TAXI
The performance will continue after a brief intermission...
13
This is **Columbia Broadcasting System!**
CBS

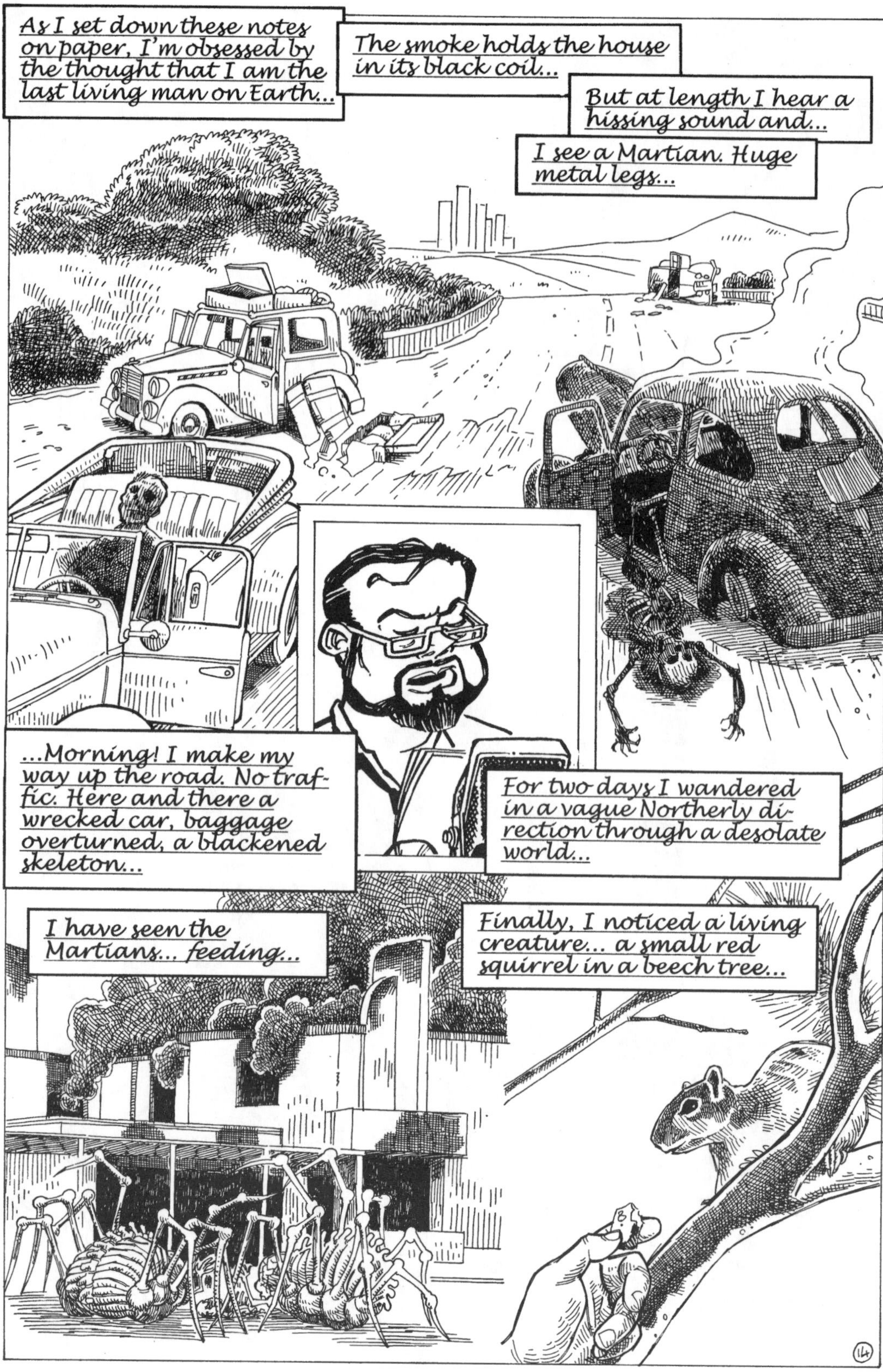
As I set down these notes on paper, I'm obsessed by the thought that I am the last living man on Earth...
The smoke holds the house in its black coil...
But at length I hear a hissing sound and...
I see a Martian. Huge metal legs...
...Morning! I make my way up the road. No traffic. Here and there a wrecked car, baggage overturned, a blackened skeleton...
For two days I wandered in a vague Northerly direction through a desolate world...
I have seen the Martians... feeding...
Finally, I noticed a living creature... a small red squirrel in a beech tree...
14

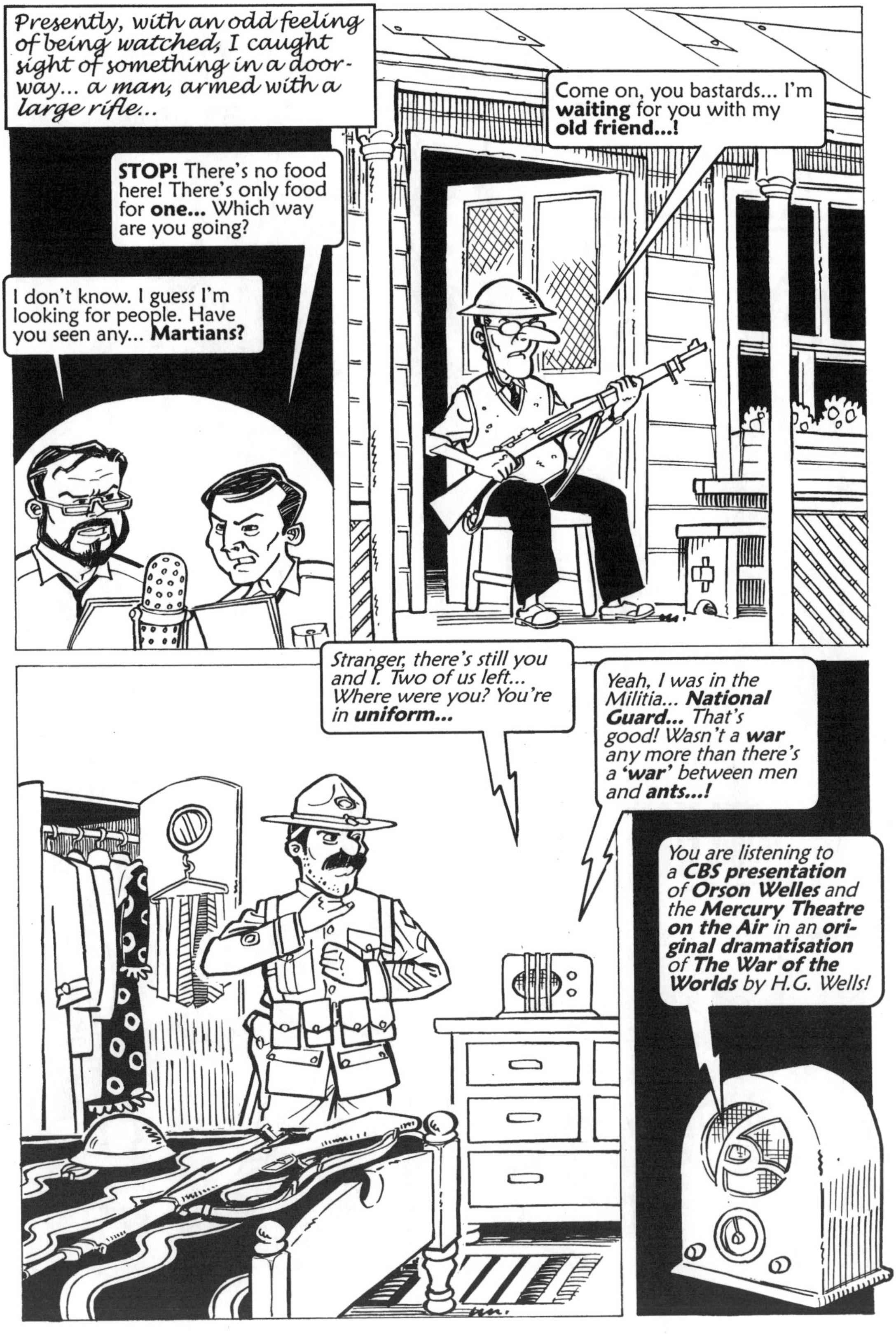
Presently, with an odd feeling of being watched, I caught sight of something in a doorway... a man, armed with a large rifle...
STOP! There's no food here! There's only food for one... Which way are you going?
I don't know. I guess I'm looking for people. Have you seen any... Martians?
Come on, you bastards... I'm waiting for you with my old friend...!
Stranger, there's still you and I. Two of us left... Where were you? You're in uniform...
Yeah, I was in the Militia... National Guard... That's good! Wasn't a war any more than there's a 'war' between men and ants...!
You are listening to a CBS presentation of Orson Welles and the Mercury Theatre on the Air in an original dramatisation of The War of the Worlds by H.G. Wells!

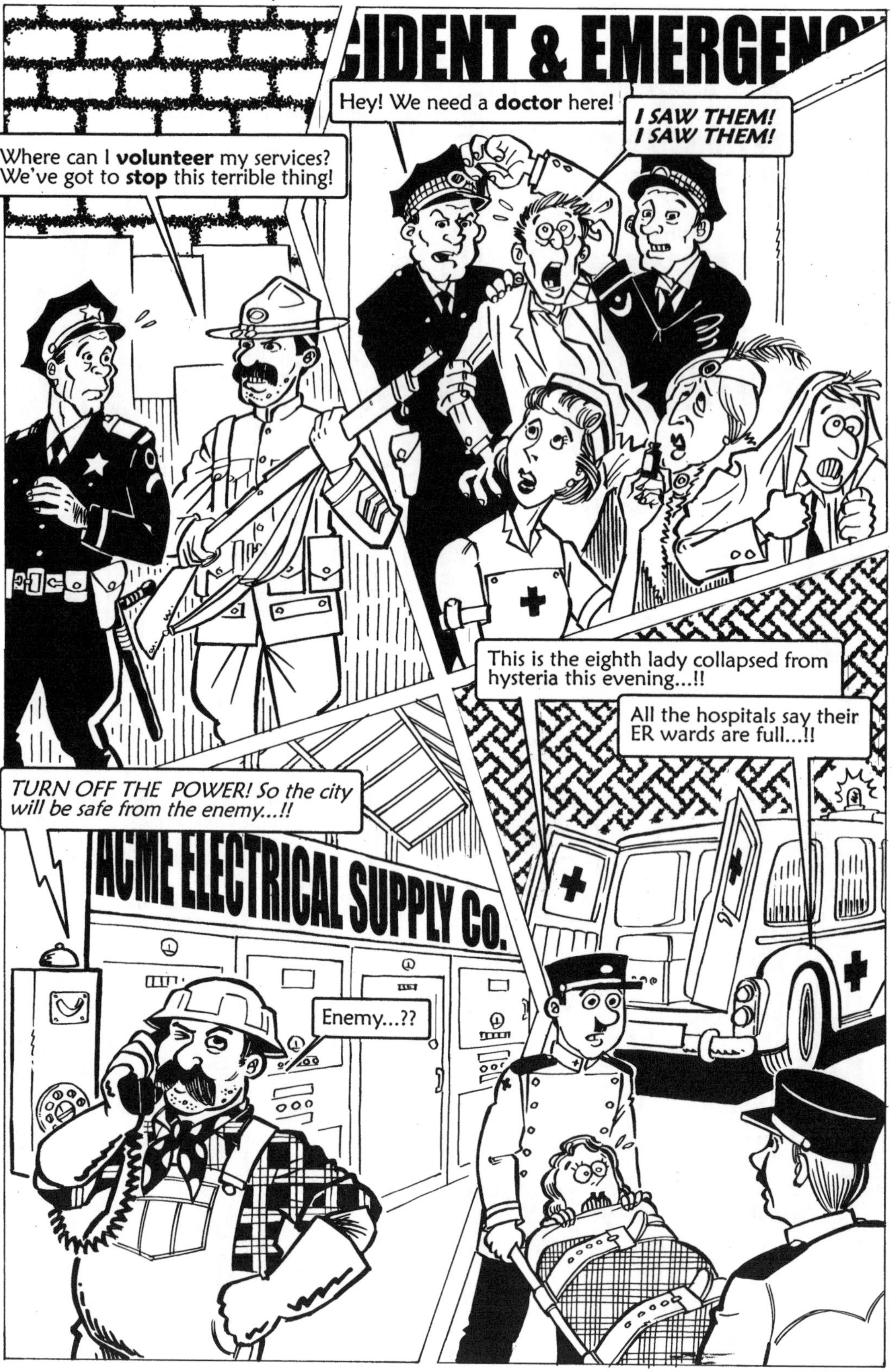
CIDENT & EMERGENC
Where can I **volunteer** my services? We've got to **stop** this terrible thing!
Hey! We need a **doctor** here!
I SAW THEM! I SAW THEM!
This is the eighth lady collapsed from hysteria this evening...!!
All the hospitals say their ER wards are full...!!
TURN OFF THE POWER! So the city will be safe from the enemy...!!
ACME ELECTRICAL SUPPLY Co.
Enemy...??

Wow! Is somebody bombing *New York??*

Hey, kid ~ switch that **radio** on, willya?

Hello, *'Daily News'* city desk... **What!?** A *Martian attack...!!?*

What are you going to **do?**

I'm going on... right under their **feet.** I got a **plan.** We **men** are **finished!** We don't **know** enough ... it isn't all of us that were made to be **wild beasts,** and that's what it's got to be. That's why I watched **you.**

"...in an original dramatisation of *The War of the Worlds* by H. G. Wells..."

Where are we to **live** when the **Martians** own the **Earth?**

It's a **radio drama!** Quick, get the **photographers!** We need to change the **first page** of the newspaper...!!

We'll live **underground...** and we'll get a bunch of **strong men** together. No **weak** ones, that rubbish... **out!**

⑰

121

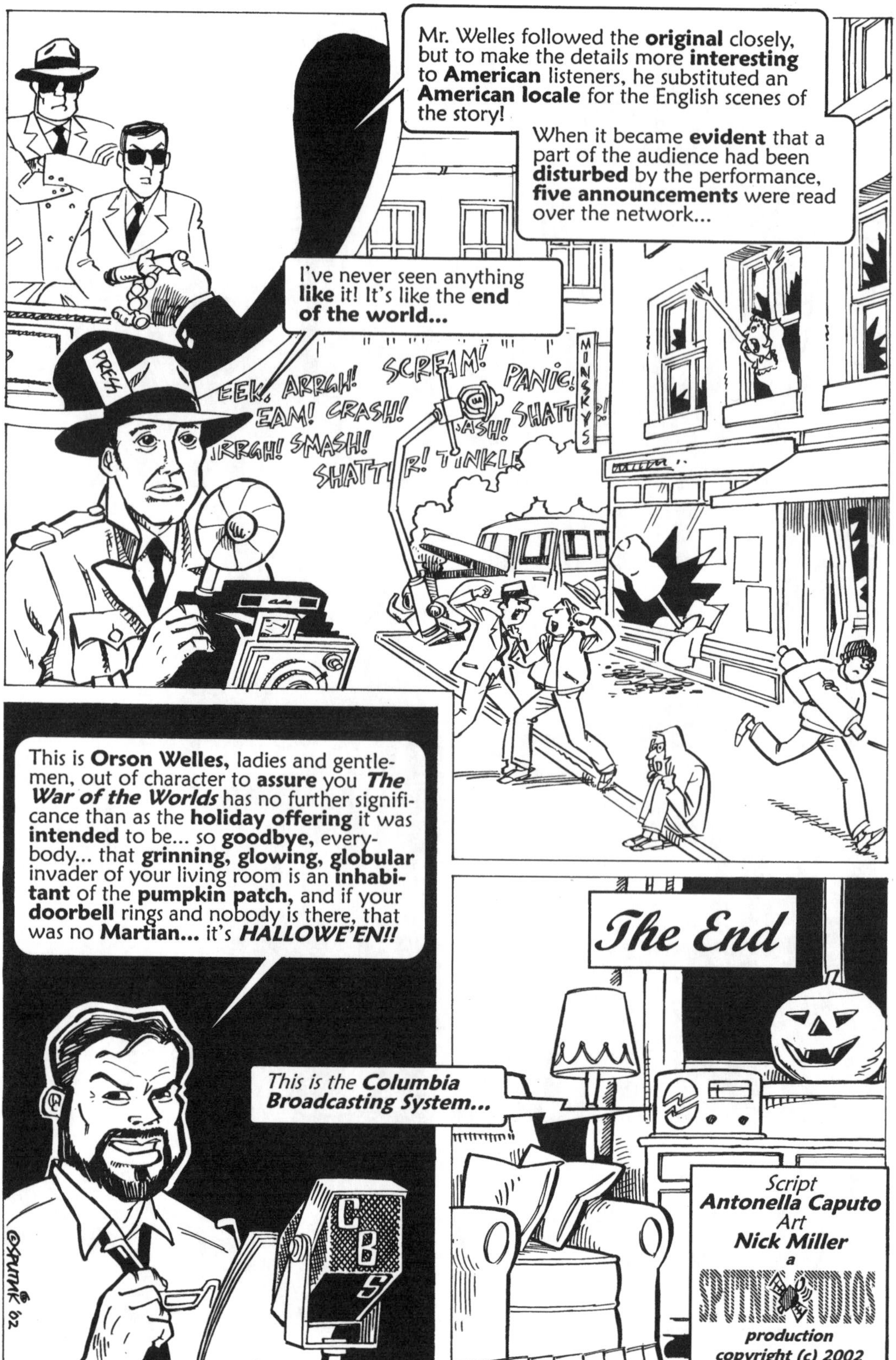
Mr. Welles followed the **original** closely, but to make the details more **interesting** to **American** listeners, he substituted an **American locale** for the English scenes of the story!
When it became **evident** that a part of the audience had been **disturbed** by the performance, **five announcements** were read over the network...
I've never seen anything **like** it! It's like the **end of the world...**
PRESS
EEK! ARRGH!
CRASH!
SMASH!
PANIC!
TINKLE
MINSKY'S
This is **Orson Welles,** ladies and gentlemen, out of character to **assure** you ***The War of the Worlds*** has no further significance than as the **holiday offering** it was **intended** to be... so **goodbye,** everybody... that **grinning, glowing, globular** invader of your living room is an **inhabitant** of the **pumpkin patch,** and if your **doorbell** rings and nobody is there, that was no **Martian...** it's ***HALLOWE'EN!!***
*This is the **Columbia Broadcasting System...***
CBS
The End
Script
Antonella Caputo
Art
Nick Miller
a
SPUTNIK STUDIOS
production
copyright (c) 2002
©SPUTNIK '02

an excerpt from # The Desert Daisy

written & illustrated by

H.G. WELLS

H.G. Wells, comic book artist? Among his many other accomplishments, Wells might be credited as one of the earliest practioners of the form in his illustrated book *The Desert Daisy.*

The book was created around 1879, when Wells was thirteen years old. At the age of seven he had broken his leg, treatment for which at the time consisted of months of lying in bed, waiting for the bones to heal. Wells began to read voraciously during and after his convalescence, and by the age of ten he had written the first of several "graphic novels." *The Desert Daisy* is the only one known to still exist. The complete hand-written and illustrated manuscript runs 102 pages, a remarkable sustained achievement for a boy of his age.

Young Bertie Wells credits the book as a collaboration between himself, as illustrator, and "The Immortal Buss," a variation of a nickname used in correspondence with his family. He tells the story of a war between the nations of the King of Clubs and the King of Spades over an incident involving a pair of torn britches, and complicated by the theft of the King's crown by the Prince Bishop.

Wells went to extremes in modeling his manuscript after a full-fledged book, including several prefaces, a table of contents, and concluding notes, as well as brief fictional book reviews or "Notices of the Press." While it is clearly a child's fairy tale, *The Desert Daisy* shows the roots of Wells' interest in war and the follies of politics, society, and religion which are explored in greater depth throughout his career.

The book was printed in a facsimile of the original manuscript in 1957 in a limited edition by the national library science honorary fraternity, Beta Phi Mu, at the University of Illinois. 🌹

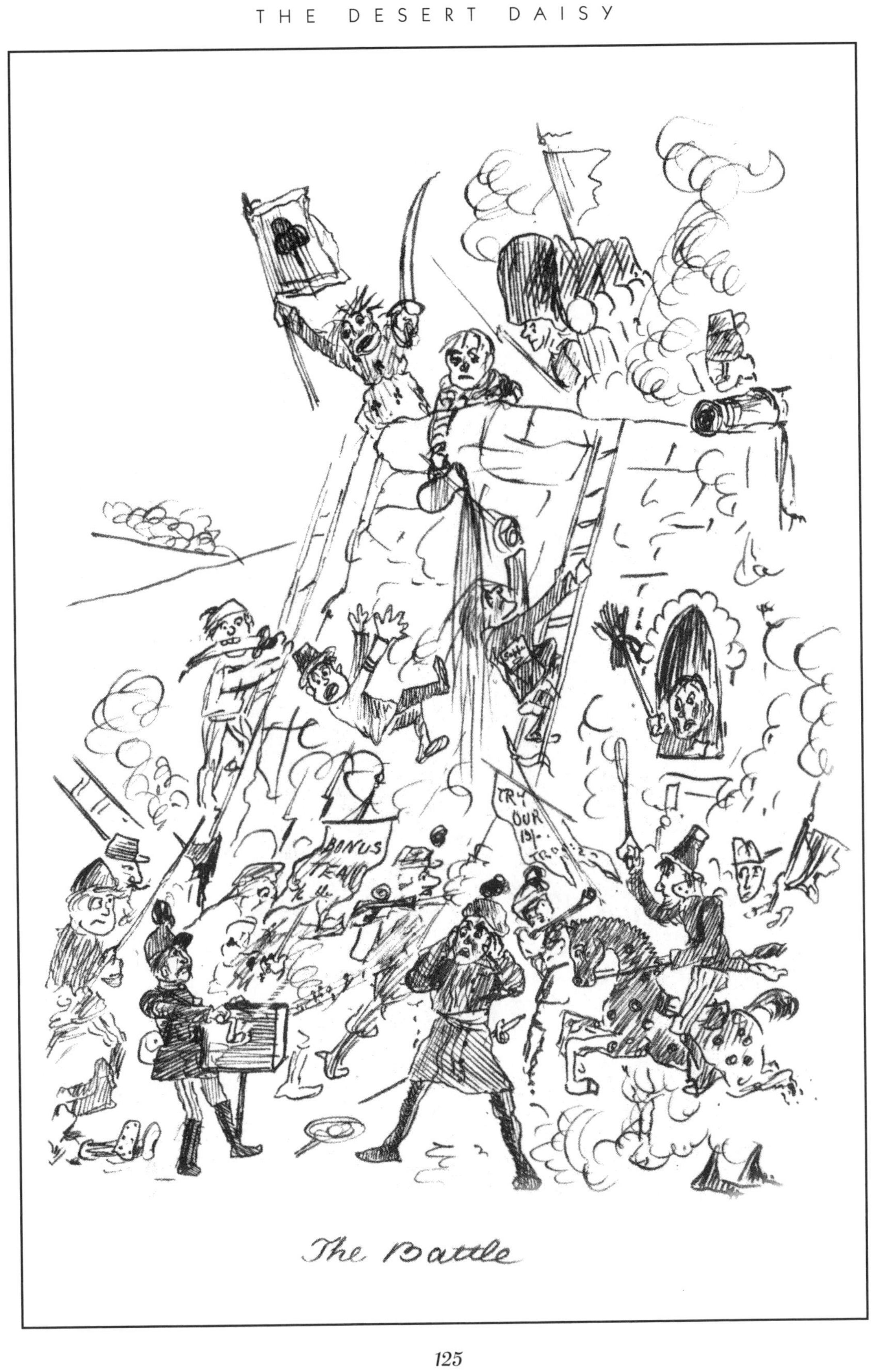
BONUS
TRY
OUR

The Battle

Le Mari Terrible

illustrated by SHAG

©2001 SHAG

Story by H.G. Wells

"You are always so sympathetic," she said; and added, reflectively, "and one can talk of one's troubles to you without any nonsense."

I wondered dimly if she meant that as a challenge. I helped myself to a biscuit thing that looked neither poisonous nor sandy. "You are one of the most puzzling human beings I ever met," I said,—a perfectly safe remark to any woman under any circumstances.

"Do you find me so hard to understand?" she said.

"You are dreadfully complex." I bit at the biscuit thing, and found it full of a kind of creamy bird-lime. (I wonder why women *will* arrange these unpleasant surprises for me—I sickened of sweets twenty years ago.)

"How so?" she was saying, and smiling her most brilliant smile.

I have no doubt she thought we were talking rather nicely. "Oh!" said I, and waved the cream biscuit thing. "You challenge me to dissect you."

"Well?"

"And that is precisely what I cannot do."

"I'm afraid you are very satirical," she said, with a touch of disappointment. She is always saying that when our conversation has become absolutely idiotic—as it invariably does. I felt an inevitable desire to quote bogus Latin to her. It seemed the very language for her.

"*Malorum fiducia pars quosque libet*," I said, in a low voice, looking meaningly into her eyes.

"Ah!" she said, colouring a little, and turned to pour hot water into the teapot, looking very prettily at me over her arm as she did so.

"That is one of the truest things that has ever been said of sympathy," I remarked. "Don't you think so?"

"Sympathy," she said, "is a very wonderful thing, and a very precious thing."

"You speak," said I (with a cough behind my hand), "as though you knew what it was to be lonely."

"There is solitude even in a crowd," she said, and looked round at the six other people—three discreet pairs—who were in the room.

"I, too," I was beginning, but Hopdangle came with a teacup, and seemed inclined to linger. He belongs to the "Nice Boy" class, and gives himself ridiculous airs of familiarity with grown-up people. Then the Giffens went.

"Do you know, I always take such an interest in your work," she was saying to me, when her husband (confound him!) came into the room.

He was a violent discord. He wore a short brown jacket and carpet slippers, and three of his waistcoat buttons were (as usual) undone. "Got any tea left, Millie?" he said, and came and sat down in the armchair beside the table.

"How do, Delalune?" he said to the man in the corner. "Damned hot, Bellows," he remarked to me, subsiding creakily.

She poured some more hot water into the teapot. (Why must charming married women always have these husbands?)

"It *is* very hot," I said.

There was a perceptible pause. He is one of those rather adipose people, who are not disconcerted by conversational gaps. "Are *you*, too, working at Argon?" I said. He is some kind of chemical investigator, I know.

He began at once to explain the most horribly complex things about elements to me. She gave him his tea, and rose and went and talked to the other people about autotypes. "Yes," I said, not hearing what he was saying.

"'No' would be more appropriate," he said. "You are absent-minded, Bellows. Not in love, I hope—at your age?"

Really, I am not thirty, but a certain perceptible thinness in my hair may account for his invariably regarding me as a contemporary. But he should understand that nowadays the beginnings of baldness merely mark the virile epoch.

"I say, Millie," he said, out loud and across the room, "you haven't been collecting Bellows here—have you?"

She looked round startled, and I saw a pained look come into her eyes. "For the bazaar?" she said. "Not yet, dear." It seemed to me that she shot a glance of entreaty at him. Then she turned to the others again.

"My wife," he said, "has two distinctive traits. She is a born poetess

and a born collector. I ought to warn you."

"I did not know," said I, "that she rhymed."

"I was speaking more of the imaginative quality, the temperament that finds a splendour in the grass, a glory in the flower, that clothes the whole world in a vestiture of interpretation."

"Indeed!" I said. I felt she was watching us anxiously. He could not, of course, suspect. But I was relieved to fancy he was simply talking nonsense.

"The magnificent figures of heroic, worshipful, and mysterious womanhood naturally appeal to her —Cleopatra, Messalina, Beatrice, the Madonna, and so forth."

"And she is writing—"

"No, she is acting. That is the real poetry of women and children. A platonic Cleopatra of infinite variety, spotless reputation, and a large following. Her make-believe is wonderful. She would use Falstaff for Romeo without a twinge, if no one else was at hand. She could exert herself to break the heart of a soldier. I assure you, Bellows—"

I heard her dress rustle behind me.

"I want some more tea," he said to her. "You misunderstood me about the collecting, Millie."

"What were you saying about Cleopatra?" she said, trying, I think, to look sternly at him.

"Scandal," he said. "But about the collecting, Bellows—"

"You must come to this bazaar," she interrupted.

"I shall be delighted," I said, boldly. "Where is it, and when?"

"About this collecting," he began.

"It is in aid of that delightful orphanage at Wimblingham," she explained, and gave me an animated account of the charity. He emptied his second cup of tea.

"May I have a third cup?" he said.

The two girls signalled departure, and her attention was distracted. "She collects—and I will confess she does it with extraordinary skill—the surreptitious addresses—"

"John," she said over her shoulder, "I wish you would tell Miss Smithers all those interesting things about Argon." He gulped down his third cup, and rose with the easy obedience of the trained husband. Presently she returned to the tea-things. "Cannot I fill your cup?" she asked.

© 2000 SHAG

"I really hope John was not telling you his queer notions about me. He says the most remarkable things. Quite lately he has got it into his head that he has a formula for my character."

"I wish *I* had," I said, with a sigh.

"And he goes about explaining me to people, as though I was a mechanism. 'Scalp collector,' I think is the favourite phrase. Did he tell you? Don't you think it perfectly horrid of him?"

"But he doesn't understand you," I said, not grasping his meaning quite at the minute.

She sighed.

"You have," I said, with infinite meaning, "my sincere sympathy—" I hesitated—"my whole sympathy."

"Thank you *so much*," she said, quite as meaningly. I rose forthwith, and we clasped hands, like souls who strike a compact.

Yet, thinking over what he said afterwards, I was troubled by a fancy that there was the faintest suggestion of a smile of triumph about her lips and mouth. Possibly it was only an honourable pride. I suppose he has poisoned my mind a little. Of course, I should not like to think of myself as one of a fortuitously selected multitude strung neatly together (if one may use the vulgarism) on a piece of string,—a stringful like a boy's string of chestnuts,—nice old gentlemen, nice boys, sympathetic and humorous men of thirty, kind fellows, gifted dreamers, and dashing blades, all trailing after her. It is confoundedly bad form of him, anyhow, to guy her visitors. She certainly took it like a saint. Of course, I shall see her again soon, and we shall talk to one another about one another. Something or other cropped up and prevented my going there on her last Tuesday.

THE *Star*

illustrated by

BRAD TEARE

Story by H.G. Wells

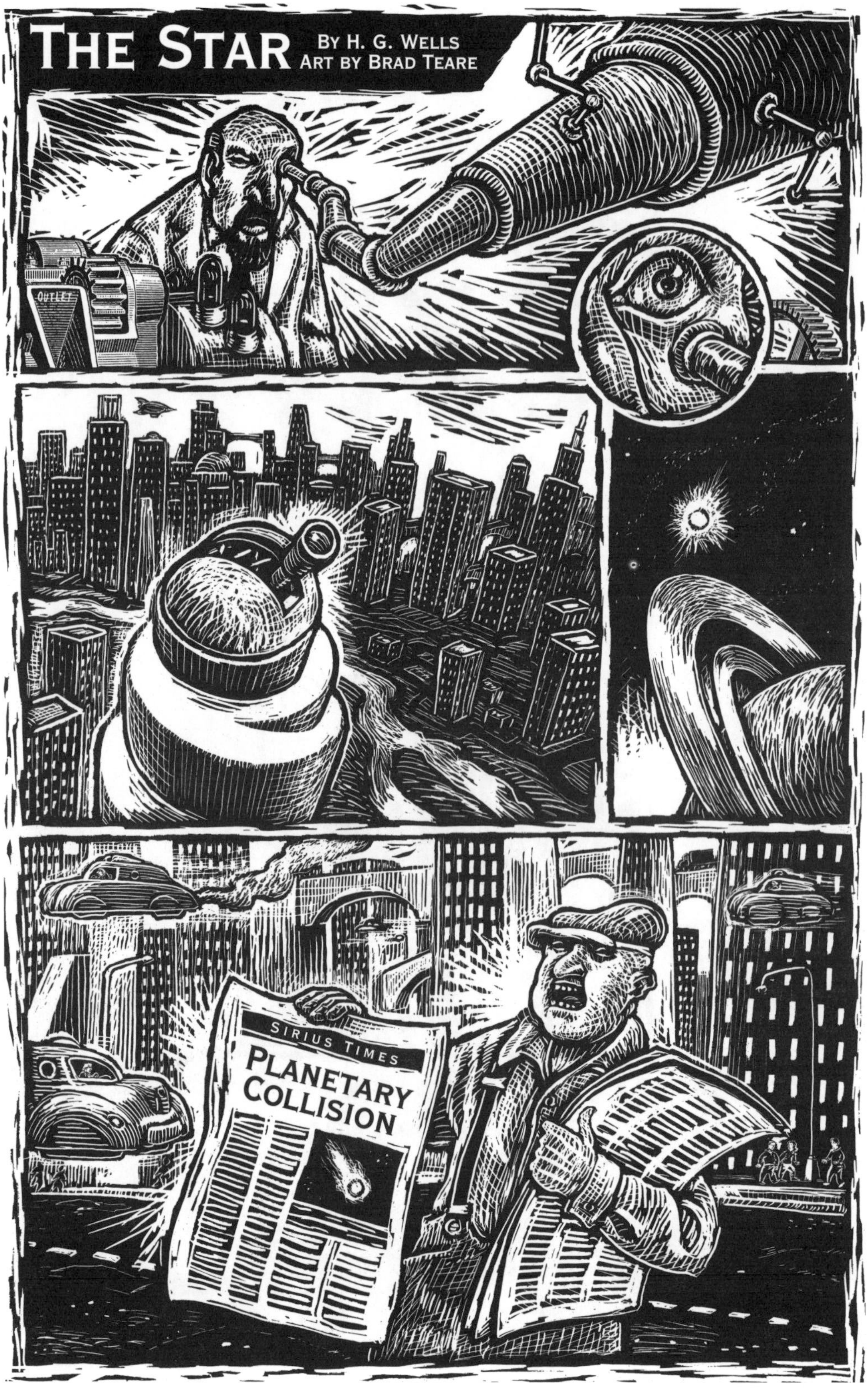
THE STAR
BY H. G. WELLS
ART BY BRAD TEARE
OUTLET
SIRIUS TIMES
PLANETARY COLLISION

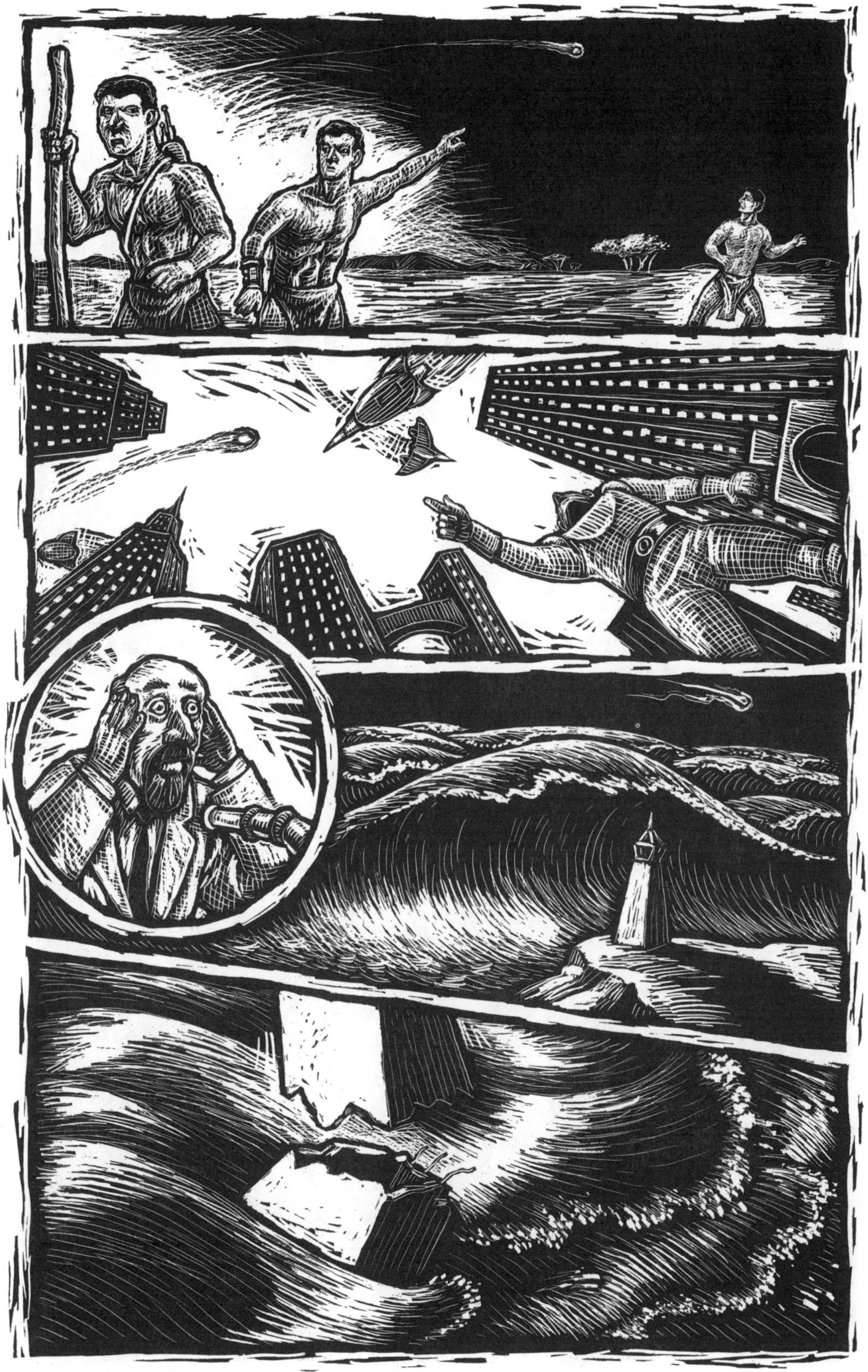

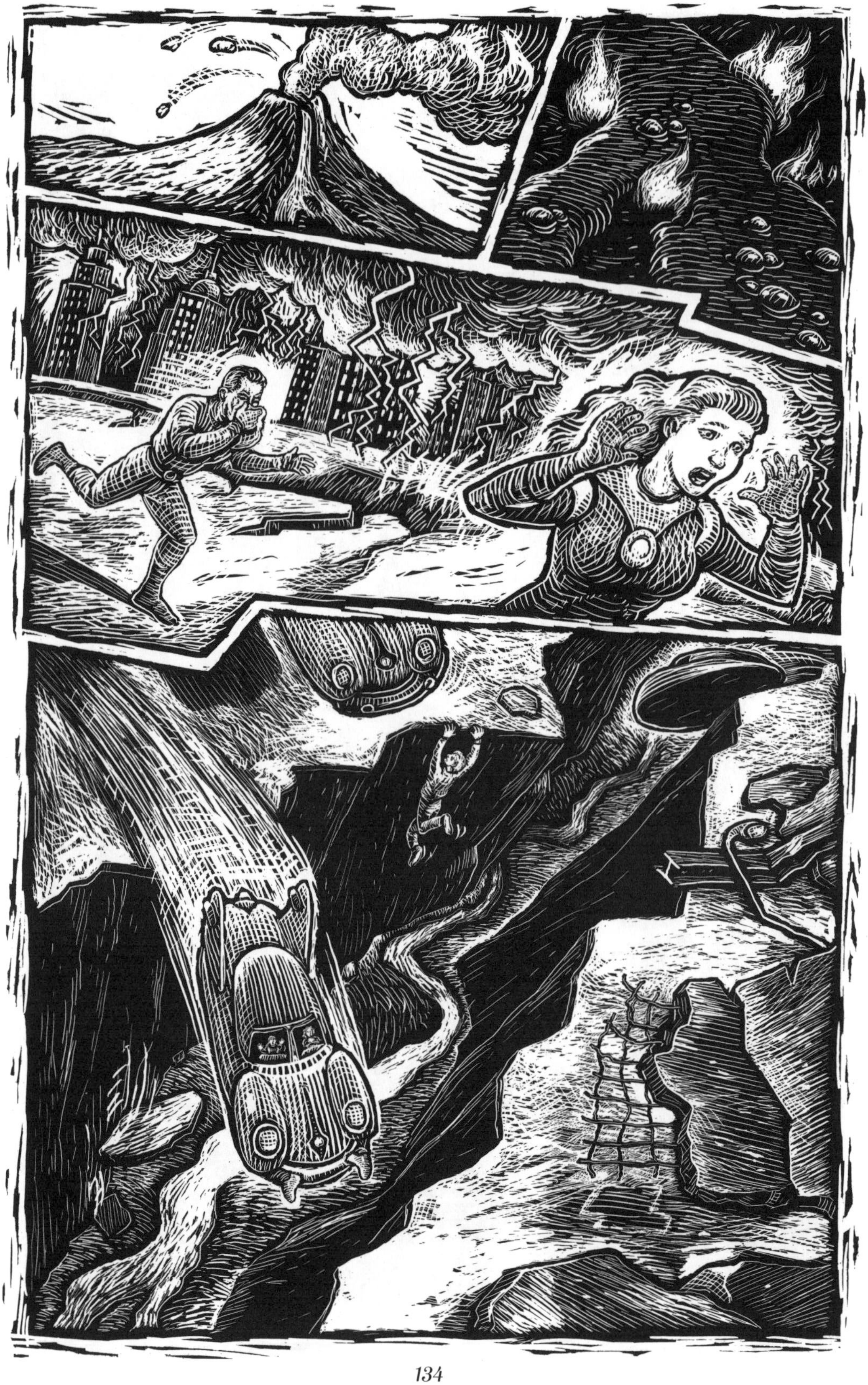

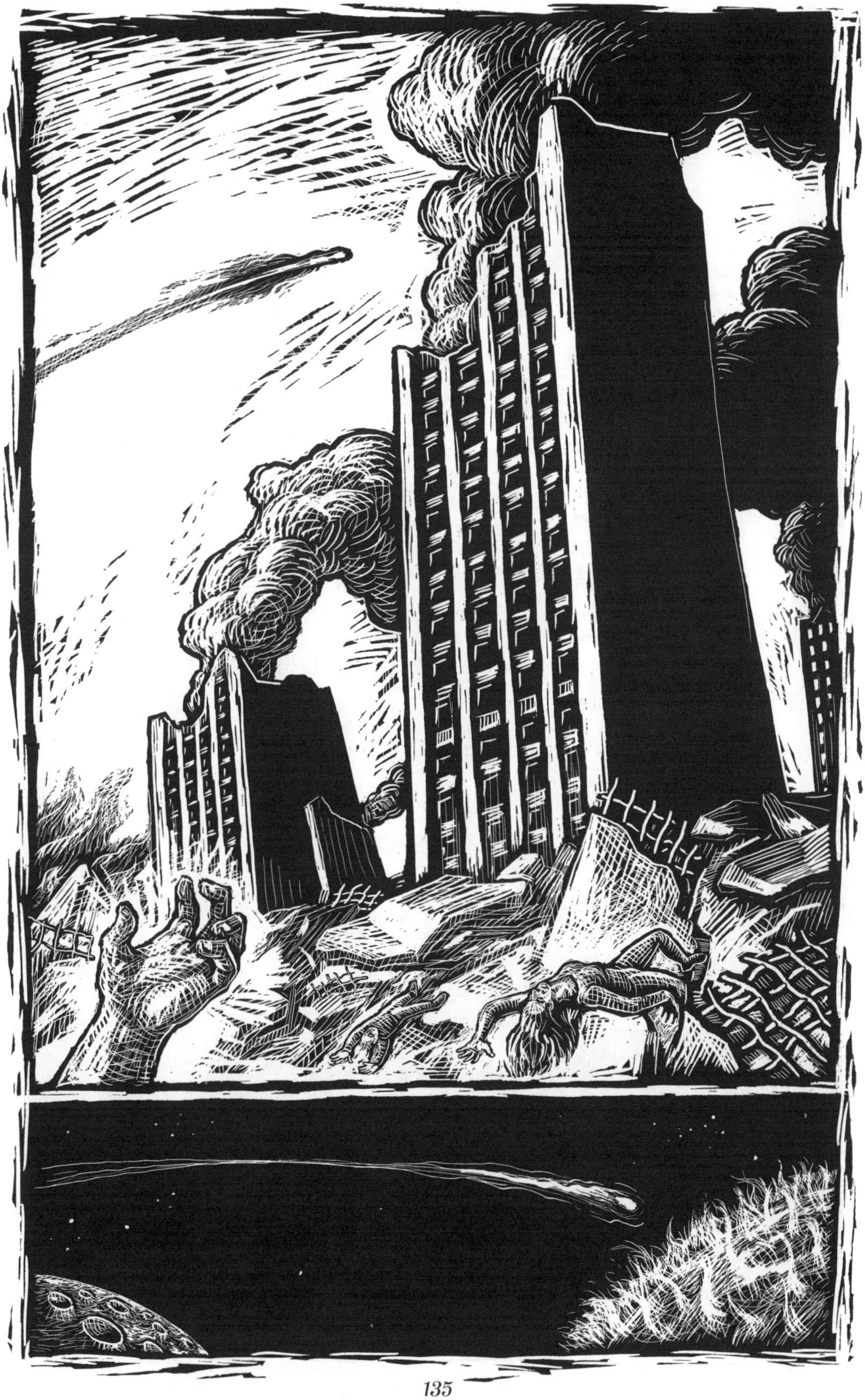

IT IS AMAZING WHAT LITTLE DAMAGE
THE EARTH HAS SUSTAINED. THE MASSES
OF THE SEAS REMAIN INTACT. THE
ONLY DIFFERENCE SEEMS TO BE A
SHRINKAGE OF POLAR ICE.

THE END

H.G. WELLS

Herbert George Wells was born to English working-class parents in 1866. At age eighteen he earned a scholarship to Imperial College, where he came under the tutelage of Darwinian scholar T.H. Huxley. Evolutionary theory strongly influenced Wells' early "scientific romances." The first of these, *The Chronic Argonauts,* was serialized in his college newspaper in 1888. Seven years later he rewrote it as *The Time Machine: An Invention,* which became the first published in a series of popular novels including *The Island of Dr. Moreau, The Invisible Man, The War of the Worlds,* and *The First Men in the Moon.* These "romances" became the foundation of modern science fiction. Their seminal influence in the field is challenged only by the French fantasist Jules Verne, who Wells claimed "can't write himself out of a paper sack." Wells briefly joined England's socialist movement and in later novels promoted socialism, feminism, and free love, which he put into personal practice. He was a leading proponent of the League of Nations and chaired the original proposal. Wells wrote numerous short stories and essays and more than one hundred fifty books, including the nonfiction *Outline of History,* which sold over two million copies. But it is his early science fiction that remains his most enduring legacy. Before his death in 1946 Wells provided his own epitaph to an interviewer: "God damn you all, I told you so."

VINCENT DI FATE *(cover)*

Vincent Di Fate has been one of the most prominent illustrators in the SF and fantasy genres for over thirty years. He has won all the major awards in his field; the Hugo, the Frank R. Paul, the Lensman, the Skylark and the Artistic Achievement Award from the Association of Science Fiction and Fantasy Artists, the last three for lifetime achievement. He has appeared on the covers of a vast number of SF magazines and books, and has produced astronomical and aerospace art for such clients as IBM, *Reader's Digest,* The National Geographic Society and NASA. He served two terms as president of the Society of Illustrators, and is a past president of the Association of Science Fiction and Fantasy Artists. Di Fate has authored three books; the most recent, *The Science Fiction Art of Vincent Di Fate,* was published by Paper Tiger Books in January, 2002. *Infinite Worlds: The Fantastic Visions of Science Fiction Art* (1997, Penguin Studio Books) is a major reference work on the history of American science fiction illustration.

Di Fate's cover painting was originally produced in 1983, but was never used until now. Vincent revised the art specifically for this volume. "My painting for *The War of the Worlds* is one of several that I've done," says Di Fate. "Most artists tend to depict the war machines moving in a shambling, stiff-legged motion, as seems to be suggested in the novel. I thought I'd try a different articulation for the legs that would suggest a swifter, more fluid kind of mobility—something more like that of a crab or spider." You can see more of Vincent Di Fate's art on his website at www.vincentdifate.com.

RICK GEARY *(page 2)*

Rick is best known for his thirteen years as a contributor to *The National Lampoon.* His work has also appeared in Marvel, DC, and Dark Horse comics, *Rolling Stone, MAD, Heavy Metal, Disney Adventures, The Los Angeles Times* and *The New York Times Book Review.* He has written and illustrated five children's books and published a collection of his comics, *Housebound with Rick Geary.* He has most recently completed the fourth in his continuing book series *A Treasury of Victorian Murder. The Mystery of Mary Rogers* (NBM Publishing, 2001) examines the famous 1841 murder which inspired Poe's *The Mystery of Marie Roget.* Rick recently created a new comics adaptation of the Sherlock Holmes story *The Copper Beeches* for *Graphic Classics: Arthur Conan Doyle,* and his version of *The Tell-Tale Heart* was a highlight of *Graphic Classics: Edgar Allan Poe.* He joined *Rosebud* as its regular feature cartoonist with Issue 22. Rick produced a complete comics adaptation of *The Invisible Man* for First Publishing's *Classics Illustrated* revival in 1991, but the illustration here was done in 2002 for this volume. You can view more of his art on the web at www.rickgeary.com.

HENRY NG *(page 4)*

Henry Ng is a native of the Rogers Park area of Chicago. "After dabbling in graffiti art, mountain biking, neurosurgery and indulging a brief dream as a Cantonese killer-for-hire,"

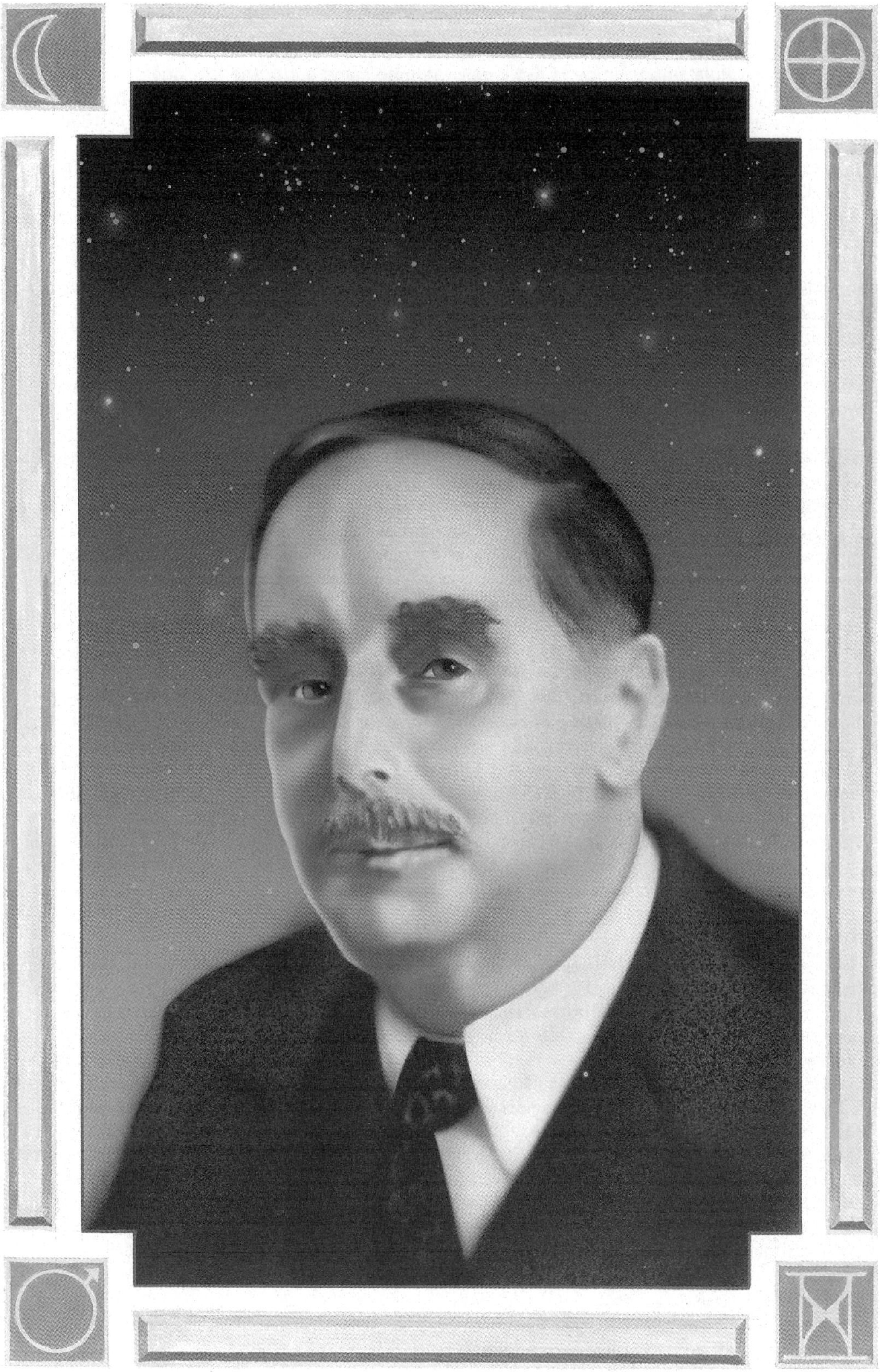

H.G. WELLS ©2002 KENT STEINE

claims Henry, "I attended the American Academy of Art, where I somehow mustered my way through the much coveted, but heavily maligned, BFA program." His comic work has appeared in the critically acclaimed *NON* comics anthology, *Bombtime for Bonzo*, and *Driver's Side Airbag*. Commerical design clients have included the Chicago Transit Authority, Eli's Cheesecake, Wilson Sporting Goods, Gary Fisher Bikes, Gilbert Paper, and the Chicago Public Art Group. Check out *www.comixwerks.com* to see more of Henry's work.

RAY VUKCEVICH *(page 5)*

Ray's short story collection *Meet Me in the Moon Room* (2001, Small Beer Press) has been nominated for the 2001 Philip K. Dick Award. The title story originally ran in *Rosebud 15*. Other short fiction has appeared in magazines and anthologies including *Fantasy & Science Fiction, Asimov's, Lady Churchill's Rosebud Wristlet, The Infinite Matrix, Talebones, Twists of the Tale* and *Pulphouse*. His first novel is *The Man of Maybe Half-a-Dozen Faces* (2000, St. Martin's Press). "I've tried to think of some pivotal literary experience in my life that would explain why I write and do what I do," says Ray, "but my awful secret is that I just make it all up." Ray lives in Oregon and works as a programmer in a university brain lab. His vampiric love story *Dead Girlfriend* appears in *Rosebud 23*.

ALEX NINO *(page 7)*

Alex Niño was born in 1940 in Luzon, the Philippines. He attended college with the intention of becoming a doctor, but soon left school to pursue his lifelong interest in art. His first comics stories were published in 1959. He synthesized the prevailing style of Filipino comics master Francisco Coching, along with influences from contemporaries Jess Jodloman, Ruben Yandoc, Alfredo Alcala and Nestor Redondo, to develop his own distinctive, though ever-changing, style. For the next fifteen years Alex illustrated over 300 stories for Filipino comics publishers. His early work is collected in the limited-edition book *Satan's Tears*. In 1971 he was introduced by Filipino artist Tony de Zuñiga to the U.S. market and DC Comics. He produced a number of exceptional stories, mostly for DC's horror anthologies, and in 1973 was contracted by publisher Vincent Fago to do comics adaptations for Fago's *Now Age Classics*. Niño moved to the U.S. in 1974, where he has since worked for every major comics publisher in the country.

Alex Niño's illustrations for *The Invisible Man* originally appeared in Fago's series published in 1974 by Pendulum Press, which has been reprinted since in its original comics-for-children form by several publishers. The version in this volume utilizes Niño's bold illustrations in a completely revised format, presented for adult readers with an abridged restoration of Wells' original text.

DAN O'NEILL *(page 40)*

In 1963 Dan O'Neill dropped out of college and started his comic *Odd Bodkins* for the *San Francisco Chronicle*. The strip was soon syndicated to over 350 papers, with a combined readership of 50 million. For seven years O'Neill proceeded to entertain readers and offend editors by satirizing religion and politics, targeting characters from Superman to Abraham Lincoln to Jesus Christ. He managed to lose 90% of the feature's sydication before finally being fired by the *Chronicle*. These strips are collected in two books, *Hear the Sound of My Feet Walking Drown the Sound of My Voice Talking* (1969) and *The Collective Unconscience of Odd Bodkins* (1973, Glide Publications). In 1970, at the height of the underground comix movement, O'Neill met four cartoonists who would form the core of his infamous comics collective,

..SOMEONE ELSE IS WRITING MY AUTOBIOGRAPHY..

The Air Pirates: Ted Richards, Gary Hallgren, Bobby London and Shary Flenniken. They produced three issues of *Dan O'Neill's Comics and Stories*, which consisted largely of satires of Disney cartoon characters, two issues of *Air Pirates Funnies* and several books by individual members of the collective. O'Neill's intent was to provoke a reaction from the Disney empire and in 1971 he succeeded. The highly-publicized court case dragged out for nine years, eventually resulting in an injunction against the Pirates and a financial judgement that was never collected by Disney. Dan returned to newspaper comics with his *Dan O'Neill* strip that continues today in T*he San Francisco Bay Guardian* and other papers. This period was collected in *Farewell to the Gipper* (1988, Eclipse Books). He is currently working on an illustrated history of The Air Pirates and another syndicated strip about contemporary families.

SHARY FLENNIKEN *(page 51)*

Seattle cartoonist, editor, author and screenwriter Shary Flenniken got her start in comics as a member of The Air Pirates. She is best known for her irreverent comic strip *Trots & Bonnie,* which originally appeared in various underground comix publications but became famous for its 1972-1990 run in *National Lampoon.* The strip features naïve teenager Bonnie, her talking dog Trots and their precocious friend Pepsi in confused and frequently sexual explorations of adulthood. Shary was profiled in *Comic Book Confidential,* the 1988 documentary film by Ron Mann. Her comics and illustrations have appeared in *Details, Premiere, Harvey* and *Mad* magazines, and books including *When a Man Loves A Walnut* by Gavin Edwards, and *Nice Guys Sleep Alone* by Bruce Feirstein. She has authored and edited *Trots and Bonnie, Sexe & Armour* and the comics anthology *Seattle Laughs* (1994, Homestead Book Co.). Shary is currently working on an illustrated writing project for national syndication and a novel that she claims is "not even remotely autobiographical." Find out more at www.sharyflenniken.com.

SKIP WILLIAMSON *(page 58)*

Artist Skip Williamson is one of the founding fathers of the underground comix movement and has been illustrating his brand of cantankerous satire for more than thirty years. A Chicago native, he began cartooning in the alternative newspapers *The Chicago Mirror* and *The Chicago Seed.* In 1968 he produced *Bijou Funnies,* one of the earliest and longest-running underground comix titles, with Robert Crumb and Jay Lynch. His style owes much to the pioneering work of *Mad* creator Harvey Kurtzman. In a 1986 interview *The Comix Journal* said, "Williamson's underground style, steeped in Art Deco flatness and crammed with calculatedly unhip scatology, carried the same joyful resonance that sparks Crumb's early work. But where Crumb's primary comics aim was introspective…Williamson took a broader look, skewering both left-wing trendiness and right-wing over-reaction…Crumb's approach may have been more personal, more artistically "legitimate," but to those of us struggling to make sense of the sociopolitical chaos, Williamson was frequently the funnier."

During the 1970s and 80s Williamson was an art director for what he calls "the carnal fleshpool of Hugh Hefner's *Playboy* magazine." In addition to numerous comics including *Gag Reflex, Naked Hostility, Pighead, Class War Comix* and *Smoot,* he has published two anthologies of his work; *Halsted Street* (1990, Kitchen Sink Press) and *The Scum Also Rises* (1998, Fantagraphics Books). Skip is now editing and assembling a 300-hundred page anthology entitled *My Bitter Agenda.* Williamson recently moved to the Atlanta area, where he is concentrating on painting large-scale canvases. His work has appeared in numerous galleries and is currently featured in *Rosebud 24.* His comics adaptation of *The Man with a Nose* features a cameo by his most famous character, the compulsive and gullible Snappy Sammy Smoot. You can see more of Skip's bitter agenda at www.thewilliamsongallery.bizland.com.

JOHN PIERARD *(page 62)*

John Pierard has had a varied career in illustration. After leaving the bosom of his beloved Syracuse University for New York City, he immediately found work in publications such as *Screw* and *Velvet Touch Magazine,* where he illustrated stories like *Sex Junky* (opening line: "*She had a face like a madonna, and I came all over it…*") In a major departure, he graduated to illustrating children's fiction including Mel Gilden's *P. S. 13* series, and various projects written and edited by noted children's author Bruce Coville. He has worked for Marvel Comics, *Asimov's Magazine,* Manhattan's Lincoln Center, and has most recently illustrated lavish editions of classic children's books for Greenwich Press. He currently resides in upper

Manhattan with his "good old dog, Annie." His adaptation of Wells' *In the Abyss* was originally done in 1989 for *The Bank Street Book of Science Fiction*.

M.K. BROWN *(page 77)*

Mary K. Brown's 1972-1981 work in *National Lampoon* first brought her public notice. Her cartoons and illustrations have also appeared in *Playboy, Atlantic Monthly, Mother Jones, The New Yorker, Arcade, Young Lust* and *Wimmin's Comics*. She has been included in *The Big Book Of New American Humor, Twisted Sisters, The New Yorker 75th Anniversary Collection* and numerous other anthologies. Her hilarious *Dr. Janice N!Godatu* animated shorts alternated with the original *Simpsons* episodes on *The Tracey Ullman Show* in 1987. MK has written and illustrated several children's books. Her first, *Let's Go Swimming With Mr. Sillypants*, received the Junior Literary Guild Award and was featured on *Reading Rainbow*. This was followed by *Sally's Room* and *Let's Go Camping with Mr. Sillypants* (1995, Crown Publishers). Current projects include *Jackknife Your Big Rig*, a cartoon collection, and an illustrated novelette called *Wolf Boy*. Of her story here, MK says, "Contributing to *Graphic Classics* has been as much a pleasure as drawing Pyecraft stuck on the ceiling was a challenge." To see more cartoons, animation and posters by MK, please visit www.benway.com/mkbrown.

NICOLA CUTI *(page 86)*

Born in Brooklyn in 1944 to first-generation Italian Americans, Nicola Cuti inherited his love of art from his father, a professional photographer. On completing his Air Force service in 1969, Nick joined eminent comics artist Wally Wood as an assistant. He later worked at Warren and DC comics, and in the early 1970s spent a notable period as assistant editor at Charlton Comics, where he co-created and scripted fan-favorite *E-Man* with artist Joe Staton. He then moved to California, where he has worked as an animation background designer for Disney, Universal, and other studios.

Cuti continued to freelance illustration for magazines including *Twilight Zone, Alfred Hitchcock* and *Amazing Stories*. He recently created a space opera, *Captain Cosmos, the Last Starveyer,* as a television pilot and a comic book with Joe Staton. Nick's *Time Machine* illustrations were originally begun fifteen years ago, and completed especially for this volume. "When I was a child I read the *Classics Illustrated* version of *The Time Machine* drawn by Lou Cameron," says Nick. "Not only did the illustrations fascinate me, but the idea that a person could build such a marvelous machine in his own basement spurred me into thinking time travel was within my reach. When Berni Wrightson came out with his beautifully illustrated version of *Frankenstein* I was inspired to dedicate myself to illustrating my own favorite novel and here are the results."

MILTON KNIGHT *(page 97)*

Milton Knight claims he started drawing, painting and creating his own attempts at comic books and animation at age two. "I've never formed a barrier between fine art and cartooning," says Milt, "growing up, I treasured Chinese watercolors, Breugel, Charlie Brown and Terrytoons equally. My childhood was during the era of 'pop art,' when fine artists were freely inspired by comics and other popular culture; I remember being captivated by these works during trips to museums and galleries in New York." Knight left home at eighteen and enjoyed a semi-homeless existence on Manhattan's waterfront before he finally landed in a Brooklyn brownstone where he spent seven waterbuggy years. He wrote and drew comics for magazines and small newspapers, illustrated record covers, posters, candy packaging and T-shirts, and occasionally exhibited his paintings. Labor on *Ninja Turtles* comics allowed him to get up a grubstake to move to the West Coast in 1991, where he worked as an animator and director on *Felix the Cat* cartoons.

"In my work," he says, "I parody the excesses of popular culture. I fight to keep my figures and backgrounds full-bodied and full of motion, to never do anything 'easily,' to always twist the figures and perspectives into going that 'extra mile.'" This is certainly the case in his illustrations for *The Temptation of Harringay*. Milt is currently illustrating magazines, exhibiting his paintings (which can be seen at www.strangetoons.com), writing and illustrating a children's book and finishing a solo ten-minute animated film.

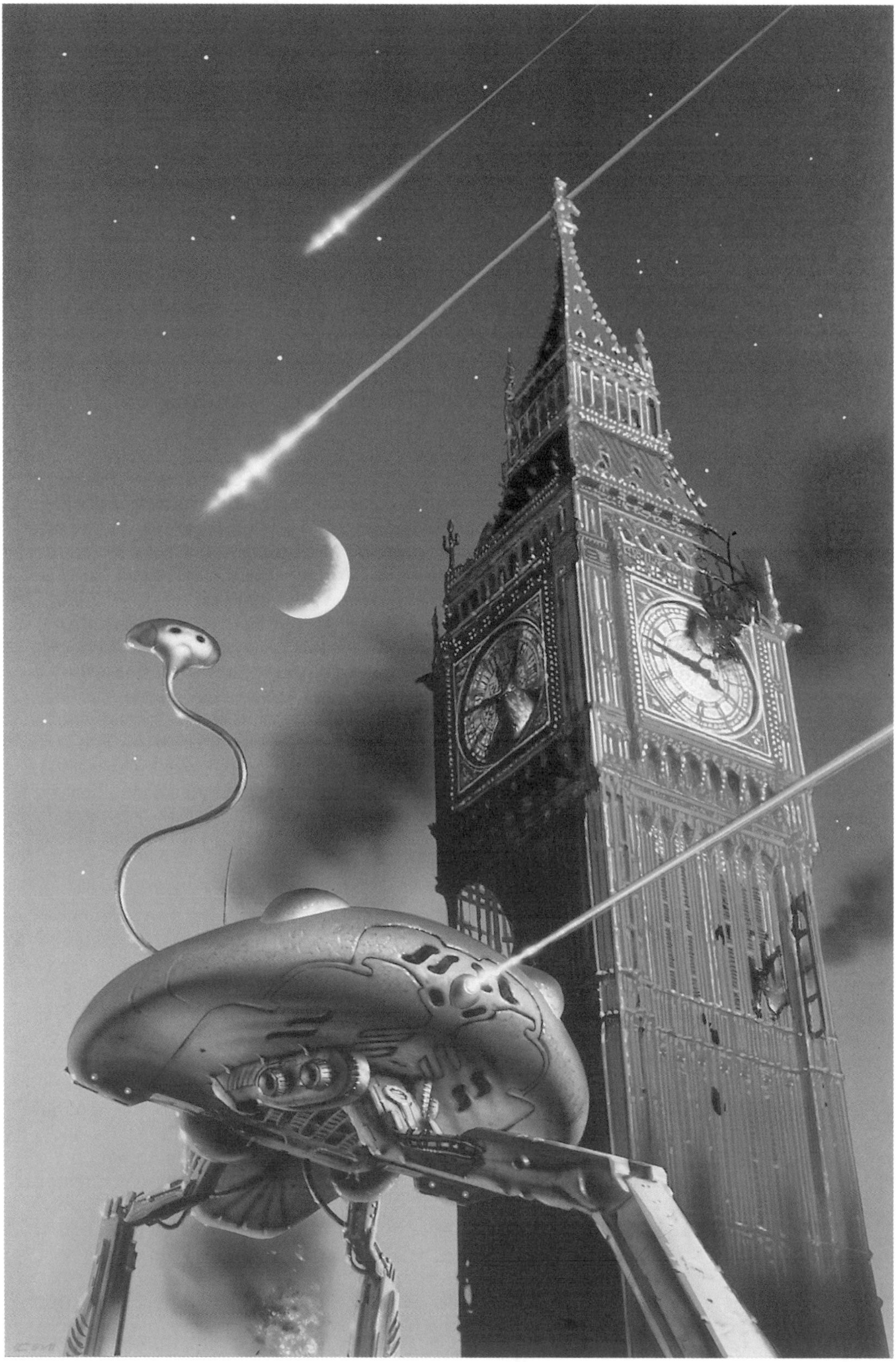

ANTONELLA CAPUTO (*page 104*)

Antonella Caputo was born and educated in Rome, Italy, and is now living in England. She studied at several different institutions, and is something of a Renaissance woman, working as an architect, archaeologist, art restorer, photographer, calligrapher, interior designer, theatre designer, actress and theatre director. She first started writing for her own amusement, but took it up seriously after being encouraged by friends. Her first published work was *Casa Montesi*, a weekly comic strip that appeared in *Il Journalino*. She has since written comedies for children and scripts for comics in Europe and the U.S., before joining Nick Miller as a partner in Sputnik Studios. Nick and Antonella have collaborated for several years, but *The War of the Worlds* is the first official Team Sputnik production.

NICK MILLER (*page 104*)

The son of two artists, Nick Miller grew up in the depths of rural Shropshire, where he learned to draw from an early age. After leaving college he worked for a while as a graphic designer, before a bout of chronic fatigue syndrome forced him to switch to cartooning full-time. Since then, his work has appeared in many publications in Britain, Europe and the U.S. including *Maps & Prints, Doctor Who Magazine, Blockheads Monthly, Mega Prize, Mega Star, 3rd Sector Magazine, Squib, Cartoon Monthly* and *The Big Issue*. He has contributed to the comics anthologies *Acne, Smut, Spit* and *Top Banana*, and to children's magazines such as *It's Wicked!, Fizzog, The Greenie, US Kids* and *Blue Moon*. His weekly newspaper comics appear in *The Planet on Sunday*. Nick shares his Lancaster, England house with two cats, a lodger and Antonella Caputo. You can see more of Nick and Antonella's work at http://www.cat-box.net/sputnik.

SHAG (*page 126*)

Josh Agle, better known as "Shag," was born in 1962 and raised in Hawaii and California. He began doing commercial design work in 1988, which he continues today, though he has scaled it back in favor of his fine arts painting. Shag's recurring themes of voodoo, devils, musicians and tiki bars are rendered in a graphic 1950s style that owes much to the work of artists Gene Deitch and Saul Bass. He is generally associated with the "lowbrow" art movement which includes artists such as Robert Williams, Mark Ryden, Todd Schorr and Mitch O'Connell and is centered around the La Luz de Jesus Gallery in Hollywood. Shag had his first solo show there in 1998. He has since exhibited in Europe, Australia and Japan as well as many U.S. cities. Shag has illustrated numerous music CDs, appeared in publications including *Time* and *Forbes* as well as art magazines like *Juxtapoz*, and has published two collections of his work, *Supersonic Swingers* (2000, Outré Gallery Press) and *Bottomless Cocktail* (2001, La Luz de Jesus Press/Last Gasp). In discussing with Josh a way for him to work *Graphic Classics* into his busy schedule, Tom Pomplun was struck by the way Shag's 1950s-style cocktail lounge paintings, executed in the 21st century, fit with Wells' story of a turn-of-the-last century tea party. Josh agreed, and another Wellsian experiment in time travel is thus presented here.

Shag is completing work for solo shows in Tokyo, Sydney, Los Angeles and Dallas, and in August the Brea Museum will host a seven-year retrospective of his work, titled *Sophisticated Misfits*. Learn more at www.shag-art.com.

BRAD TEARE (*page 131*)

Utah artist Brad Teare maintains a career as both illustrator and fine arts painter. Clients include *The New York Times, Fortune* and Random House, where he has created book covers for authors such as James Michener, Ann Tyler, and Rafael Yglesias. Teare's comics creations have appeared in *Heavy Metal* and the *Big Book* series from Paradox Press. He is currently Senior Designer at *The Friend* magazine. Brad is now turning his graphic novel *Cypher* (excerpted in *Rosebud 20*) into a screenplay. You can check out his work at www.st45.com/cypher.

"I was intrigued by the H.G. Wells story *The Star* mostly for its dissimilarities to my storytelling style," he says. "That which Wells tends to elaborate, I abbreviate. I wanted to take his story and compress it into its minimal shape creating a black hole to pull the viewer through the experience quickly. Controlling the viewer's rate of information assimilation is very important to me. A novel demands a fixed amount of time. A painting is assimilated instantly. The comics medium fluctuates between these two poles of time and space."

KENT STEINE (page 138)

Kent Steine is a classically trained illustrator who has been painting pretty girls for over twenty years. He began his career producing advertising and editorial illustration and has done cover art for over fifty periodicals. His first major exposure as a glamour artist came in 1992 with the creation of his *Hollywood Glamour* limited edition prints, produced by Siabur Graphics. These contemporary images helped reestablish an interest in classic pinup and glamour art. Kent's pinup illustrations have appeared in numerous magazines, and have been published in the form of prints, lithographs, posters, trading cards and calendars. As an author, Steine has written *The J.C. Leyendecker Collection* and *Billy DeVorss Pinup.* He was a contributing writer to *Step-By-Step Graphics* and now to *Illustration* magazine. He is currently working on a series of images for a promotional campaign with fitness expert Cyndi Targosz. More of Kent's art can be seen at www.kentsteine.com.

CHRIS MOORE (page 142)

English artist Chris Moore is one of the premier illustrators of science fiction working today. He was born in Rotherham, South Yorkshire in 1947 and always wanted to be a commercial artist. He attended Maidstone College of Art and the Royal College of Art in London, and in 1972 formed Moore Morris Ltd. with Michael Morris, where he illustrated book, magazine and record covers. In 1974 he did his first SF covers, for books by Alfred Bester and Philip K. Dick. He has specialized in the field ever since, and the roster of his covers reads like a *Who's Who* of the SF elite, including Isaac Asimov, Larry Niven, Frederick Pohl, Anne McCaffrey, Clifford D. Simak, Kurt Vonnegut, J.G. Ballard, Arthur C. Clarke and Samuel R. Delany. His painting of *The War of the Worlds* was done for the cover of a 1998 Orion volume that combined *The War of the Worlds* and *The Time Machine* in one book. "I very much wanted the atmosphere to be both British and Wellsian," states Chris. "I thought it would be nice to have Big Ben standing as a timepiece along with the Martian tripod, giving a presence to both themes in the same image." Chris Moore's art is featured in *Rosebud 23* and in *Fantasy Art Masters* (1999, Watson-Guptill). *Journeyman*, a collection of his work, was published in 2000 by Paper Tiger. His website is at www.illust.demon.co.uk.

JIM NELSON (back cover)

Jim Nelson's work has appeared in fantasy role-playing games, books and magazines. He has been represented in the juried annual *Spectrum: The Best in Contemporary Fantastic Art* as both an artist and art director. Jim is also an award-winning graphic designer and a die-hard football fan. He claims artistic influences from Rembrandt to Wrightson, and contemporary fantastic artists like De Es Schwertberger and Zdzislaw Beksinski rank among his favorites. Jim lives and works in Chicago. He is currently working on Wizards of the Coast's popular *Magic: The Gathering* card game and is also involved in projects for White Wolf, *Weekly Reader* and *Riotminds.*

For his back cover painting Jim chose a scene from *The Time Machine* in which the Time Traveller and Weena stumble upon a hall full of huge, inexplicable machines in the Palace of Green Porcelain. "I loved the idea of those machines," says Jim, "which represent a technology beyond the understanding of the Time Traveler, rotting away in a ruined museum in the far future."

TOM POMPLUN

Tom is a graphic artist and lifetime science fiction and comics fan. He has designed and produced *Rosebud*, a journal of fiction, poetry and illustration since its debut in 1993. *Graphic Classics* is his first venture into publishing. Tom is currently collaborating with a staggering thirty-one great artists on *Graphic Classics: H.P. Lovecraft*, due in November 2002.